Entrepreneurs' Search for
Sources of Knowledge

Other titles in Foundations and Trends® in Entrepreneurship

The Evolution of Hidden Champions as Niche Entrepreneurs
Erik E. Lehmann and Julian Schenkenhofer
ISBN: 978-1-63828-258-7

Entrepreneurship in the Long-Run: Empirical Evidence and Historical Mechanisms
Michael Fritsch and Michael Wyrwich
ISBN: 978-1-63828-108-5

Minority Entrepreneurship 2.0
Timothy Bates
ISBN: 978-1-63828-048-4

From the Metaphor to the Concept of the Entrepreneurial Journey in Entrepreneurship Research
Tõnis Mets
ISBN: 978-1-63828-016-3

Student Entrepreneurship: Reflections and Future Avenues for Research
Bart Clarysse, Philippe Mustar and Lisa Dedeyne
ISBN: 978-1-63828-012-5

Lumps, Bumps and Jumps in the Firm Growth Process
Alex Coad
ISBN: 978-1-68083-960-9

Entrepreneurs' Search for Sources of Knowledge

Albert N. Link

University of North Carolina at Greensboro

anlink@uncg.edu

the essence of knowledge

Boston — Delft

Foundations and Trends® in Entrepreneurship

Published, sold and distributed by:
now Publishers Inc.
PO Box 1024
Hanover, MA 02339
United States
Tel. +1-781-985-4510
www.nowpublishers.com
sales@nowpublishers.com

Outside North America:
now Publishers Inc.
PO Box 179
2600 AD Delft
The Netherlands
Tel. +31-6-51115274

The preferred citation for this publication is

A. Link. *Entrepreneurs' Search for Sources of Knowledge.* Foundations and Trends®
in Entrepreneurship, vol. 19, no. 7, pp. 590–663, 2023.

ISBN: 978-1-63828-296-9
© 2023 A. Link

Foundations and Trends® in Entrepreneurship
Volume 19, Issue 7, 2023
Editorial Board

Editorial Scope

Topics

Foundations and Trends® in Entrepreneurship publishes survey and tutorial articles in the following topics:

- Nascent and start-up entrepreneurs
- Opportunity recognition
- New venture creation process
- Business formation
- Firm ownership
- Market value and firm growth
- Franchising
- Managerial characteristics and behavior of entrepreneurs
- Strategic alliances and networks
- Government programs and public policy
- Gender and ethnicity

- New business financing:
  - Business angels
  - Bank financing, debt, and trade credit
  - Venture capital and private equity capital
  - Public equity and IPOs
- Family-owned firms
- Management structure, governance and performance
- Corporate entrepreneurship
- High technology:
  - Technology-based new firms
  - High-tech clusters
- Small business and economic growth

Information for Librarians

Foundations and Trends® in Entrepreneurship, 2023, Volume 19, 4 issues. ISSN paper version 1551-3114. ISSN online version 1551-3122. Also available as a combined paper and online subscription.

Contents

Entrepreneurs' Search for Sources of Knowledge

Albert N. Link

Virginia Batte Phillips Distinguished Professor, University of North Carolina at Greensboro, USA; anlink@uncg.edu

ABSTRACT

The primary purpose of this monograph is to explore the search process for knowledge used by entrepreneurs and entrepreneurial firms in pursuit of new opportunities, new product innovation opportunities in particular. Understanding the search for and the use of informational sources is important at both the behavioral level and at the policy level. At the behavioral level, such an understanding expands the existing literature and research scope of scholars related to research on innovative activity, and innovative activity is important because it is a fundamental source of economic growth. At the policy level, such an understanding about sources of knowledge enhances the use of public-sector innovation initiatives in pursuit of economic growth.

The second purpose of this monograph is to present empirical evidence about the sources of knowledge that entrepreneurs and entrepreneurial firms actually use (and actually do not use) in an effort to allow observed behavior to inform future economics and management theory about the search for and use of knowledge sources. The theoretical literature on this topic is limited and often uninformed by the actual behavior of entrepreneurs and the boundary constraints they

Albert N. Link (2023), "Entrepreneurs' Search for Sources of Knowledge", Foundations and Trends® in Entrepreneurship: Vol. 19, No. 7, pp 590–663. DOI: 10.1561/0300000127.

face. The empirical evidence presented might begin to provide a foundation for additional theoretical advancements on the use of alternative sources and their economic and entrepreneurial implications for the firm. With such a foundation, working backwards to how a firm identified, searched for, and decided to use such sources might be possible.

And, the third purpose of this monograph is to generate new and more complete empirical efforts to construct databases and to conduct analyses—empirical analyses and case studies—related not only to entrepreneur's and entrepreneurial firm's search for and use of sources of knowledge but also to measure the trends in the impacts of their use.

1

Introduction

Human life has always been lived on the edge of precipice. Human culture has always had to exist under the shadow of something infinitely more important than itself. If men had postponed the search for knowledge and beauty until they were secure, the search would have never begun. We are mistaken when we compare war with "normal life." Life has never been normal.

— C.S. Lewis, *The Weight of Glory*

As the epigraph above suggests, the search for knowledge is profoundly important, and the implications from the epigraph are that one should strive to embrace an effort to understand and appreciate the process of searching for knowledge.

If one generalizes from the wisdom of C.S. Lewis to the behavior of entrepreneurs and entrepreneurial firms, it is perhaps not a big leap to seek to understand how their search for knowledge—new knowledge—has affected their behavior; how and why a search occurred and what and when have been the implications from that search.

However, the pages that follow do not provide definitive answers to these questions; rather what follows points a reader in a direction from which he/she might begin to think about how to address these issues given that the related academic and policy literature (hereafter referred to as the extant literature) is limited not only in its volume but also in its focus on the antecedents and consequences of the search for sources of knowledge.

Regarding the pages that follow, the purpose of this monograph is three-fold, and these three purposes are intertwined.

The first and broader purpose of this monograph is to explore the search process for knowledge by entrepreneurs and entrepreneurial firms in pursuit of new opportunities, new product innovation opportunities in particular as explained in later sections.[1] Understanding the search for and the use of information sources is important at both the behavioral level and at the policy level. At the behavioral level, such an understanding expands the existing literature and research scope of scholars related to their research on innovative activity, and innovative activity is important because it is a fundamental source of economic growth. At the policy level, such an understanding enhances the use of innovation initiatives promulgated by policy makers in their pursuit of levers to pull to enhance economic growth.

Understanding the use of information sources at the policy level has contemporary relevance. As one example, consider university technology transfer. Much if not most of university research is funded by the public sector and the transfer of resulting technologies to the private as well as the public sector has social benefits as enumerated in and incentivized through the Bayh-Dole Act of 1980.[2]

Figure 1.1 illustrates a model of university technology transfer. The model has 12 steps or processes as summarized in Table 1.1.[3]

Figure 1.1, as well as the extant literature discusses in detail how technology is transferred from a university often through patents; however, conspicuously absent from the university technology transfer literature

---

[1] By intent, I am not restricting my arguments to the search for only new knowledge. Existing knowledge can be rediscovered, and it may complement new knowledge to enhance outcomes.

[2] A detailed discussion of the Bayh-Dole Act of 1980 as an example of public-sector entrepreneurship is in Hayter *et al.* (2018).

[3] For a discussion of alternative technology transfer classifications see Goel and Rich (2005).

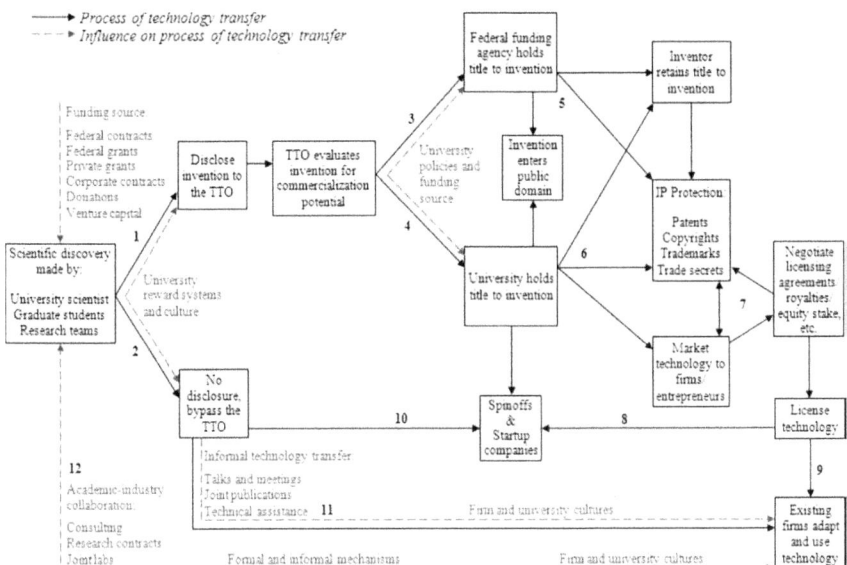

Figure 1.1: A model of university technology transfer.

Source: Bradley *et al.* (2013, p. 621).

is a discussion of how technology-related ideas or technology-related knowledge enters a university. What sources of knowledge do faculty rely on to enhance their ideas? My point is that there are knowledge flows into and out of a university, and the same is true for federal research laboratories and entrepreneurial firms. Understanding both knowledge flows is, I believe, paramount to a complete understanding of the two-way technology transfer process which is critical to understanding the search for knowledge and the net benefits from alternative sources of that knowledge.

One should not interpret this first purpose statement to imply that there is a void of scholarship that focuses on the search for and use of knowledge. On the contrary, there is such a literature but it is limited in volume as well as in scope, and it is only on occasion motivated by a theoretical model or by theoretically constructed hypotheses. And, only on occasion, does this literature go beyond the simple identification of knowledge sources to explore what entrepreneurial characteristics drive

Table 1.1: Annotated processes associated with university technology transfer as illustrated in Figure 1.1

Process 1	The inventor can choose to disclose his/her invention to the university's technology transfer office (TTO).
Process 2	The inventor can choose not to disclose his/her invention, bypassing the TTO.
Process 3	The university can decline to retain title to the invention; the federal funding agency can then request title to the invention.
Process 4	The university can retain title to the invention.
Process 5	The university requests the title to the invention and lets it enter the public domain, effectively ending the technology transfer process; it allows the inventor to retain title to the invention, as long as the university approves; the inventor is then free to file his/her own application for IP protection; he/she requests the title to the invention and files an application for IP protection, typically a patent.
Process 6	In some cases, it is decided early on that a spinoff or startup is the best way to develop the invention; in other cases, the university markets the technology to firms or entrepreneurs that can develop the technology; the university may also begin the process of acquiring IP protection in the form of patents, copyrights, trademarks, trade secrets, etc.; the university may, with the funding agency's approval, allow the inventor to retain title to the invention; if the invention is not federally funded, it may be allowed to enter the public domain; this outcome typically occurs when the invention is unlikely to have significant commercial value, or there is no market interest or need for the invention.
Process 7	The invention can be marketed before IP protection is acquired, that is, if the university wants to gauge market interest before investing significant time and resources to protecting the invention; or, if the invention seems especially promising, the university might choose to apply for patents, copyrights, etc. before or even as they are marketing it to potential investors; the university could successfully market the invention, lock in an interested firm or entrepreneur, and begin licensing negotiations before the IP protection process is completed; if the federal funding agency holds title to the invention, its next step is to file patent applications; similarly, if the inventor is permitted to retain title, he/she will likely seek IP protection before taking steps to commercialize and develop his/her invention.

Continued.

Table 1.1: Continued.

Process 8	If the technology has been licensed to an entrepreneur, such as the inventing faculty member or an outside party, a spinoff or startup company is established around the invention.
Process 9	If the technology has been licensed to an existing firm, the firm then adapts and uses the typically embryonic technology.
Process 10	A spinoff or a startup company being established that utilizes the knowledge passed on from the university scientist.
Process 11	The scientist's discovery, idea, or knowledge being adapted and used by an existing firm.
Process 12	The university scientist and the firm developing the invention often maintain a continued working relationship by means of academic–industry collaboration; the firm and university cultures must be favorable toward maintaining a partnership and engaging in technology transfer activities in order for collaborations to be successful; academic–industry collaboration can involve consulting, research contracts, the establishment of joint labs, and other partnerships between the university and the firm.

Source: Bradley *et al.* (2013, pp. 620–625).

the search for the knowledge and what the entrepreneurial implications are that consequently result from the search.

The second purpose of this monograph is to present empirical evidence about the sources of knowledge that entrepreneurs and entrepreneurial firms actually use (and actually do not use) in an effort to allow observed behavior to inform economics and management theory about the search for and use of knowledge. The theoretical literature on this topic is limited and often uninformed by the actual behavior of entrepreneurs and the boundary constraints they face. The empirical evidence presented in the following sections might begin to provide a foundation for additional theoretical advancements on the use of alternative sources and their economic and entrepreneurial implications for the firm. With such a foundation, working backwards to how a firm identified and searched for and decided to use such sources might be possible.

The third purpose of this monograph is to generate new and more complete empirical efforts to construct databases and to conduct analyses—empirical analyses and case studies—related not only to entrepreneur's and entrepreneurial firm's search for and use of sources of knowledge but also to measure the trends in the impacts of their use. It is my hope that the exploratory analyses presented in the sections that follow motivate scholars in these directions.

The remainder of this monograph is organized as follows. In Section 2, I suggest the bones of a model of entrepreneurial behavior—an individual entrepreneur or an entrepreneurial firm—that is sufficiently broad so that others might use it to study new dimensions of innovative behavior that go beyond the exploratory empirical analyses that I am able to offer in this monograph. The model that is offered relies on selected insights and arguments within the extant literature; the entire body of literature that is broadly defined to be related to sources of knowledge is not the focus of this monograph and is thus not reviewed herein.[4]

---

[4]This monograph departs from the traditional literature review published in *Foundations and Trends in Entrepreneurship* in the sense that it uses aspects of the existing literature to motivate new research on theoretical models about the search for and use of alternative sources of knowledge and to motivate new research and empirical analyses of the consequences of the use of adopted knowledge.

In Section 3, I describe the AEGIS database from which the data that are used herein to explore the model are presented in Section 2. The AEGIS database is arguably the most complete database dedicated exclusively to European entrepreneurial firms; knowledge-intensive innovative entrepreneurial (KIE) firms in particular. The units of observation in the database are KIE firms and their founders. As defined by Malerba and McKelvey (2019, p. 558):

> ...knowledge-intensive innovative entrepreneurship, shortened as KIE...provides a modern view of entrepreneurship that links the intense use of knowledge by the new ventures with a high innovative activity related to the economy and markets...KIE firms are defined as new learning organizations that use and transform existing knowledge and generate new knowledge in order to innovate within innovation systems.

The KIE firm data described in this section provide some behavioral information related to the use of alternative sources of knowledge. To acknowledge the cultural aspects of the search for knowledge, I describe alternative measures of entrepreneurial experience on a country by country basis, on an industrial sector by industrial sector basis, and on a technology sector by technology sector basis.

In Section 4, I rely on information in the AEGIS database to describe alternative sources of knowledge and a KIE firm's expressed value of usefulness of each source of knowledge in pursuit of new product innovation opportunities.

In Section 5, I rely on information in the AEGIS database to construct a measure of the experience base that resides in a KIE firm's founders.

In Section 6, I rely on information in the AEGIS database to describe alternative measures of a KIE firm's pursuit of product innovation opportunities.

In Section 7, I explore the relationship between a KIE firm's experience base (Section 4) and the *ex post* valuation of the alternative sources of knowledge that have already been used (Section 4). The behavioral model in Section 2 suggests that an entrepreneur's experience, or the overall level of experience embodied in an entrepreneurial firm, will determine the order of search in alternative knowledge-embedded areas. Unfortunately, the information in the AEGIS database (or in any database about which I know) does not describe the order of search but rather it describes a KIE firm's *ex post* assessment of the knowledge sources that have already been searched.

Section 8 is the first of two sections that explores new product innovation opportunities in terms of a KIE firm's use of alternative sources of knowledge and the professional experience embodied in a KIE firm. These relationships are explored descriptively in this section. In Section 9, these relationships are explored in a multivariate manner. Neither of these sections is to be viewed as a complete presentation of econometric-based analysis of covariates of new product innovation. Rather, these sections represent only the tip of a theoretical and empirical iceberg which is intended to point researcher on ways to motivate the expansion of theoretical scholarship on the antecedents of the use of alternative sources of knowledge as well as to motivate additional empirical analyses related to the consequences of the use of alternative sources of knowledge.

Section 10 expands on the multivariate analyses in Section 9 through the introduction of a so-called nature variable related to the gender of a KIE firm's founders in contrast to the so-called nurture variable about the professional experience embodied in a KIE firm's founders as previously considered in Sections 8 and 9.

Section 11 concludes the monograph with a survey of the conclusions from the empirical analyses in the previous sections. My hope is that these conclusions will serve as both a salvo and a roadmap for future research related to entrepreneurs' search for sources of knowledge and use of that knowledge.

2

Letting the Literature Set the Stage

2.1 Perception and Action

There is a rich, but limited, literature that relates to entrepreneurs' search for sources of knowledge. That literature might be segmented in terms of where a search for knowledge sources is to occur and how a search for knowledge sources is to be focused or conducted. The decision of where to search generally takes place before, or perhaps at the same time, as the decision of how to focus or conduct a search.

Laursen and Salter (2006) defined 16 sources for knowledge, and those 16 sources are grouped by the authors into four categories: market sources, institutional sources, other sources, and specialized sources.[1] Potentially, there are at least two ways to think about each of their 16 sources. Each source could represent a unique search area, which I refer to herein as A_i,[2] or in a specifically defined search area there could be a number of the 16 sources. One might think about the existence of search areas in general terms or, in an effort to relate the arguments

---

[1] See Table 1 in Laursen and Salter (2006, p. 139).

[2] Examples of the ith knowledge-embedded source to be searched by an entrepreneur or an entrepreneurial firm will follow in the subsequent sections. For examples in the literature see Audretsch *et al.* (2023).

that follow to the extant literature, one might think about each one of the Laursen and Salter sources ($i = 1$–16) as a unique search area.

In which area should an entrepreneur search first?[3] Following Radner and Rothschild (1975), an entrepreneur will first search that area for which he/she perceives that there is the greatest measure of knowledge relevant to his/her search objectives. And herein, and in much of the literature on sources of knowledge, an entrepreneur's objectives are defined to be the identification of new product innovation opportunities. The sequence of any subsequent searches is based on the same criterion of the identification of relevant knowledge for new product innovation opportunities.[4] Of course, this search criterion raises a question of how an entrepreneur perceives the presence of relevant knowledge in a search area.

Perception has long been attributed to an entrepreneur as being a self-defining characteristic. Hébert and Link (2009), through their trace of the intellectual history of who an entrepreneur is and what he/she does, arrived at a synthetic definition of an entrepreneur as one who *perceives* an opportunity and, in the face of uncertainty, one who has the ability *to act* on that perception.

The ability of an entrepreneur to perceive new product innovation opportunities from having successfully identified not only a search area but also a relevant knowledge-embedded source within the identified search area and having acted on that perception through an action, is assumed to be related to his/her experiences.[5]

---

[3]I thank Maksim Belitski for pointing out to me that a contrast of the behavior incumbent firms compared to seasoned firms is limited in the theoretical literature. Seasoned entrepreneurs may think differently about how to search for knowledge to maximize the propensity to innovate and explore new markets, while for incumbents it could be knowledge which allows them to stay in existing markets to continue growing. Unfortunately, the data used below all pertain to nascent entrepreneurial firms.

[4]Radner and Rothschild (1975) use the symbol $U_i(t)$ to refer to the identified amounts of or usefulness of product innovation opportunities, where i indexes the search areas and t indexes the search dates. $U_i(t) > U_i(t+1)$.

[5]Relatedly, see Guerrero and Peña-Legazkue (2013) on the relationship between experience and corporate venturing. See also Goel and Nelson's (2018) discussion of process innovations.

The importance of perception in the identification of an opportunity is not a new topic for discussion.[6] Perception is a defining characteristic of an entrepreneur.[7] And, the importance of perception has long been recognized by the early scholars in the broadly defined field of entrepreneurship as I note by the following acknowledgements (and these acknowledgements were foundational for the construction of the Hébert and Link, 2009 synthetic definition presented above).[8]

Friedrich von Wieser (1851–1926), who was a disciple of Carl Menger (1840–1921), wrote that an entrepreneur (von Wieser, 1927, p. 324):

> ... must possess the quick perception that seizes new terms in current transactions as his affairs develop; [and] he must possess the independent forcefulness to regulate his business according to his views.

A von Wieser entrepreneur must have the courage to accept risk and to be driven forward by his/her ability to create an opportunity.[9]

A number of other scholars have identified risk taking as an important trait of an entrepreneur (Hébert and Link, 2009), but more to the point, von Wieser's views about the entrepreneurial trait of perception portend future business successes, such as new product innovations.

---

[6]Along with my virtual colleague, David Audretsch, we first examined the nexus between sources of knowledge and entrepreneurial activity in 2019 in *Sources of Knowledge and Entrepreneurial Behavior* as referenced below. Since then, my thoughts on this topic have broadened.

[7]I thank James Cunningham for reminding me that opportunity and perception of opportunity is contextually bounded. This is a point that I mention below in terms of the search for knowledge in sequential areas of opportunity.

[8]I thank Maksim Belitski for reminding me that much of the previous research on entrepreneurial perception defines this perception as the ability to execute intended behavior, often referred to as self-efficacy (Krueger *et al.*, 2000).

[9]However, there is a paucity of knowledge about the concept of uncertainty and risk that exist in many aspects of economic life and how entrepreneurs use their judgment to accept but also embrace risk and uncertainty to innovate. Due to rational calculations, the incumbent firms that create knowledge cannot determine if the ideas are good or not. Incumbents use of information is that it is characterized by risk. Incumbent firms can calculate risk to make their decisions. Entrepreneurs, on the contrary, accept risk and embrace uncertainty to create new ventures and commercialize new to market products (Audretsch and Belitski, 2021).

Fritz Machlup (1902–1983), whose ideas about entrepreneurship were influenced by Friedrich Hayek (1889–1992), realized that individuals acquire knowledge differently, and the cost of acquiring knowledge is related to an individual's differential abilities (Machlup, 1980, p. 179):

> Some alert and quick-minded persons, by keeping their eyes and ears open for new facts and theories, discoveries and opportunities, perceive what normal people of lesser alertness and perceptiveness, would fail to notice. Hence new knowledge is available at little or no cost to those who are on the lookout, full of curiosity, and bright enough not to miss their chances... [10]

While Machlup does not explicitly mention risk being associated with action that is driven through perception, he, like von Wieser, is implicit about an entrepreneurial spirit being embodied in an entrepreneur perhaps through nature as much as through nurture.

Israel Kirzner (1930–), who was a student of Ludwig von Mises (1881–1972) and who remains as an influential force in the Austrian school of thought, realized that (Hébert and Link, 2009, p. 117):

---

[10]While many scholars agree with Machlup (1980) on the importance of the aspiration that knowledge gives to an individual who has their eyes open to embrace new opportunities, the characteristics embedded in knowledge (e.g., complexity, heterogeneity, scarcity) will result in costs for searching, identifying, transferring, and adapting it to market needs in order to offer new opportunities to businesses by innovating and creating new ventures (Audretsch and Belitski, 2020, 2023). Given that the objective of an entrepreneur is not only to identify market opportunities and utilize knowledge but also to turn it into products and services, there is a cost associated with access to new knowledge or generating it internally. More specifically, the properties of knowledge—scarcity, limited availability, appropriability, or lack thereof—will explicitly result in an effort, subject to elements of uncertainty, required by an entrepreneur to transform the information and data collected from the context into sensible knowledge based on skills, experiences, and education, and then turn it into innovation, which can disrupt the existing products and services in the market.

...time and uncertainty may alter the form of action called entrepreneurship but they do not change the entrepreneur's essential function.[11, 12]

The dynamic, multiperiod nature being associated with the timing and uncertainty of economic activity was the basis for Kirzner's wider view (Kirzner, 1985, pp. 63–64):

> In the single-period case alertness can at best discover hitherto overlooked current facts. In the multiperiod case entrepreneurial alertness must include the entrepreneur's perception of the way in which creative and imaginative action may vitally shape the kind of transactions that will be entered into in future market periods.

Perception of an opportunity leads, for an entrepreneur, to act on that perception in the face of uncertainty. Ludwig von Mises (1881–1972) wrote (1949, pp. 253, 254):

---

[11]I thank Maksim Belitski for pointing out to me that in addition to altering the form of action by entrepreneurs, the type of knowledge entrepreneurs access—such as knowledge spillover versus formal R&D collaboration, alliances, coopetition, and others—shapes the type of outcomes an entrepreneur might expect. This includes exploiting existing opportunities, or exploring new products and markets and creating new products that disrupt the market, and enabling a first-mover advantage. Entrepreneurial function varies according to different types of knowledge available to entrepreneurs, such as basic versus applied knowledge, explicit versus implicit knowledge, and tacit versus codified knowledge. These forms of knowledge are used at different phases of entrepreneurial activity. The value of different sources of knowledge, which are embedded in a specific context is not fixed over the entrepreneurship lifecycle, change over time. By pursuing a specific source of knowledge, an entrepreneur therefore is implicitly selecting the final outcome. This choice of knowledge source does not change the essential function of the entrepreneur in the market but rather it alters the strategic and functional ability of knowledge application. This, in turn, affects the speed of innovation, the development of market pathways, product and service commercialization, and market entry.

[12]Foss and Klein (2012) recently challenged the notion of entrepreneurial opportunities in their book titled *Organizing Entrepreneurial Judgment: A New Theory of the Firm*. Therein they rebuild Knight's judgment-based view by conceptualizing that judgmental decision-making takes place under market uncertainty. Authors discuss when, how, and why entrepreneurs would combine heterogeneous assets to create new knowledge and new products to pursue economic profit.

...the outcome of action is always uncertain. Action is always speculation. [Thus,] the term entrepreneur [means the] acting man [is] exclusively seen from the aspect of uncertainty inherent in every action.

In the summary words of Hébert and Link (2009, p. 98):

People of action who perceive and react to knowledge do so in various ways; each internalizes the public good in potentially a different way. The leader distances himself from the manager by virtue of his aptitude. According to Joseph A. Schumpeter (1883–1950), leadership aptitudes mean that "some are able to undertake uncertainties incident to what has not been done before; [indeed]...to overcome these difficulties incident to change of practice is the function of the entrepreneur" (Schumpeter, 1928, p. 380).[13]

The essential point is that risk usually means a quantity susceptible to measurement while uncertainty is not. In other words, whereas risk is measurable, it can be described by a distribution function. Incumbent firms can calculate risk to make their decisions. Uncertainty is neither measurable nor quantifiable. Entrepreneurs judge opportunities created by uncertainty and use available knowledge to generate profits as well as to lessen the risk caused by environmental uncertainties. Knight, 1921, p. 20) argued:

It is this "true" uncertainty, and not risk, which forms the basis of a valid theory of profit and accounts for the divergence between actual and theoretical competition.

Returning to the question about which search area to search first, there is an important relationship within the extant literature about the activities that define a search for knowledge. March (1991) noted that in models of rational choice there is a balance between the exploration for

---

[13]The leader distinguishes himself/herself from the manager by way of his/her thinking, such as causal thinking (goal-driven) versus effectual thinking, which can be influenced by the availability of knowledge, skills, and capabilities of entrepreneurs and teams (Sarasvathy, 2001).

knowledge and the exploitation of knowledge.[14] Leventhal and March (1993, p. 105) offered the following definitions of these two concepts:[15]

> [E]xploration [is] the pursuit of new knowledge, of things that might come to be known. ... [E]xploitation [is] the use and development of things already known.

Based on perception as being a defining characteristic of an entrepreneur, and a characteristic that perhaps defines which area an entrepreneur will search first for relevant knowledge about new product innovation opportunities, one might wonder where an entrepreneur learns to be perceptive. Is alertness and quick-mindedness, in the sense of Machlup (1980), an aspect of nature or of nurture?

Epistemologists frequently reflect on the writings of John Locke, and thus they argue that perception comes in part from nurture (but at the same time not denying that it could also come in part from nature). Audretsch and Link (2019) began their book on sources of knowledge with excerpts from Locke's most famous treatise, *An Essay Concerning Human Understanding*, first published in 1689 (dated 1690). Locke's emphasis was on the genesis of ideas; one's own source of knowledge (Locke, 1996, p. 33):[16]

> Every man being conscious to himself, that he thinks, and that which his mind is employed about whilst thinking being the *ideas*, that are there, 'tis past doubt, that men have in their minds several *ideas ... All ideas come from sensation or reflection.*

---

[14]"[M]aintaining an appropriate balance between exploration and exploitation is a primary factor in system survival and prosperity" (March, 1991, p. 71).

[15]"An organization that engages exclusively in exploration will ordinarily suffer from the fact that it never gains the returns of its knowledge. An organization that engages exclusively in exploitation will ordinarily suffer from obsolescence" Leventhal and March (1993, p. 105).

[16]"If, in the history of epistemology, any sources of knowledge deserve to be called the classical basic sources, the best candidates are perception, memory, consciousness (sometimes called introspection), and reason (sometimes called intuition). Some writers have shortened the list under the heading, 'experience and reason' " (Audi, 2002, p. 72).

Regarding sensation, Locke emphasized the perception of things, and understanding entrepreneurial behavior is tantamount to understanding one's sources for perception (Locke, 1996, pp. 33–34):

> [O]ur senses, conversant about particular sensible objects, do *convey into the mind* several distinct *perceptions* of things, according to those various ways, wherein those objects do affect them: and thus we come by those *ideas* we have of *yellow, white, heat, cold, soft, hard, bitter, sweet*, and all those which we call sensible qualities, which when I say the senses convey into the mind, I mean, they from external objects convey into the mind what produces there those *perceptions*. This great source, of most of the *ideas* we have, depending wholly upon our senses, and derived by them to the understanding, I call *SENSATION*.

And regarding reflection, (Locke, 1996, p. 34):

> [T]he other fountain, from which experience furnishes the understanding with *ideas* is the *perception of the operations of our own minds* within us, as it is employed about the *ideas* it has got; which operations, when the soul comes to reflect on, and consider, do furnish the understanding with another set of *ideas*, which could not be had from things without: and such are, *perception, thinking, doubting, believing, reasoning, knowing, willing*, and all the different actings of our own minds; which we being conscious of, and observing in ourselves, do from these receive into our understandings, as distinct *ideas*, as we do from bodies affecting our senses. This source of *ideas*, every man has wholly in himself: and though it be not sense, as having nothing to do with external objects; yet it is very like it, and might properly enough be called internal sense. But as I call the other *sensation*, so I call this *REFLECTION*, the *ideas* it affords being such only, as the mind gets by reflecting on its own operations within itself.

Sensation and reflection are the "fountains of knowledge" (1996, p. 33) from which ideas spring, but Locke perceived that one's experiences are the fundamental precursor (Locke, 1996, p. 33):

> Let us then suppose the mind to be, as we say, white paper, void of all characters, without any *ideas*; how comes it to be furnished? Whence comes it by that vast store, which the busy and boundless fancy of man has painted on it, with an almost endless variety? Whence has it all the materials of reason and knowledge? To this I answer, in one word, from *experience*; in that, all our knowledge is founded; and from that it ultimately derives itself. Our observation employed either, about *external sensible objects* [i.e., sensations], *or about the internal operations of our minds, perceived and reflected on by ourselves* [i.e., reflection], *is that, which supplies our understandings with all the materials of thinking.* These two are the fountains of knowledge, from whence all the *ideas* we have, or can naturally have, do spring.

It seems to me that early contributions to the extant literature on sources of knowledge might be viewed collectively as inferring that an entrepreneur's perception about the opportunity to find relevant knowledge is what guides him/her to decide which area to search first, and an entrepreneur's ability to perceive opportunity derives from his/her experiences.[17] Contemporary literature, or at least parts of it, seems to be of that same opinion.

---

[17]I have written about experiences in other venues, and here I draw directly from those writings to emphasize what appears to be a long-lived understanding that ideas (and I claim perception of opportunities) come from experiences. Some excerpts from *Invention, Innovation and U.S. Federal Laboratories* (Link, 2020, pp. 4–5) follow: "Albert Einstein who is quoted to have said: 'The only source of knowledge is experience'... Theodore Schultz, recipient of the Nobel Memorial Prize in Economic Sciences in 1979, argued that if experiences influence one's abilities, then the economic value of one's experiences is related, at least in some part, to one's educational background (Schultz, 1975). Building on this perspective, Fritz Machlup later wrote that formal education is only one source of knowledge; knowledge is also gained experientially and at different rates by different individuals. Individuals can accrue knowledge from their day to day experiences, which 'will normally induce reflection, interpretations, discoveries, and generalization...' (Machlup, 1980,

2.2   Experience and Where to Search for Knowledge

Locke would argue that the search for knowledge is based on one's experiences. Audretsch and Link (2019) have represented a similar antecedent and consequence of a search for knowledge as: *Experience* → *Knowledge* → *Entrepreneurial Behavior.*

There is no calculus involved in the Locke or in the Audretsch and Link approach to the search for knowledge. Simply, an entrepreneur's experiences will lead him/her to the optimal A_1 and then to a second area, if needed, and so on.[18]

The more contemporary literature is less sanguine about hypothesizing about the location and scope of the search for knowledge, and at the same time more cautious about exploring for related characteristics. In fact, to the best of my knowledge, absent from the literature are applied studies (including case studies) that describe the calculus used by entrepreneurs in deciding where to search first, second, and so on. There are several important papers that hint at a motivating factor for this search sequence, and from those hints one might glean what is driving whatever calculus an entrepreneur does use.

For example, Li *et al.* (2013, p. 894) refer to the choice of where to search by referring to a so-called search selection using the phrase:

> ...[the area] which focuses on the location managers select to direct their attention during search.

Li *et al.* aptly characterize this element of literature in terms of whether the search is "local or distant,"[19] "narrow or broad," or "familiar

---

p. 179)...Steven Johnson, the author of the New York Times bestseller *Where Good Ideas Come From*, set forth the following related point of view (2010, pp. 35–36): Good ideas are not conjured out of thin air; they are built out of a collection of existing parts, the composition of which expands (and, occasionally, contracts) over time...[T]he history of cultural progress is, almost without exception, a story of one door leading to another door, exploring the palace one room at a time."

[18]See Leyden and Menter (2018, 2022). They focus on the concept of knowledge cross-fertilization. Entrepreneurs select complementary areas of knowledge that might give them the best return (through synergies of respective knowledge areas).

[19]See also Stuart and Podolny (1996) and Rosenkopf and Nerkar (2001).

or unfamiliar."[20] These authors posit testable hypotheses based on the following proposition (2013, p. 897):

> [O]pportunities to discover novel, salient, and vivid informa-
> tion and knowledge through unfamiliar, distant, and diverse
> search selection are important because searchers are more
> likely to pay attention to such information, use it to discover
> new combinations, and to help replace obsolete knowledge
> in order to develop new products.

Using information from writings in the popular press related to new product innovation opportunities—what I assume to be the firm's objective function—Li *et al.* (2013) find that the more information that managers have about a search area (i.e., terrain source diversity) the more effective the search is in terms of acquiring information that leads to a greater number of introduced product innovations. Relatedly, Jung and Lee (2016) argue that the search for original knowledge compared to ordinary knowledge is more likely to lead to a breakthrough innovation. Criscuolo *et al.* (2018, p. 115) advocate the adoption of a "combination of knowledge sources" rather than a sequential search of A_1 then A_2, and so on. How managers acquire such information about relevant knowledge sources is not identified by Li *et al.* (2013), and neither is how managers prioritize the information in hand.[21]

In contrast to Li *et al.* (2013), Katila and Chen (2008) posit that firms that are unsuccessful in identifying a search area are those that do little more than mimic what their competitors do.

2.3 Experience and How to Search Effectively for Knowledge

Having identified a search area, A_1, the entrepreneur's challenge is to identify relevant knowledge within that area and assess its relevance to his/her search objectives. Assessment, followed by exploitation, involves the perception of opportunity; but, there is uncertainty associated with

---

[20]Li *et al.* (2013) gives literature references to each dichotomous choice.

[21]Katila (2002) makes the case that the firm or the firm's management should rely on recent or new knowledge rather than old knowledge. See also Billinger *et al.* (2021) on the complexity of the search process.

any action that is based on perception, and there is uncertainty about the relevance of such action on the desired realization of the search objectives.

It follows that the realization of the entrepreneur's search objectives, that is the effective performance, P, of the entrepreneur's identification of relevant new product innovation knowledge, will be a function of the characteristics of search area A_1, or any subsequent search areas, A_2 through A_i, as well as a function of the entrepreneur's effectiveness, γ, in identifying and exploiting relevant knowledge.[22] Thus, for the ith search area:[23]

$$P_i = f(A_i, \gamma) \qquad (2.1)$$

Once in search area, A_1, the entrepreneur must decide on search depth as well as search scope, both of which embody an element of uncertainty. Following Katila and Ahuja (2002, p. 1183):

> Firms can vary in their degree of use and reuse of their existing knowledge, just as they can vary in their exploration of new knowledge. We call the first dimension, which describes how deeply a firm reuses its existing knowledge, search depth. We call the second dimension, which describes how widely a firm explores new knowledge, search scope.

But, the more experienced the entrepreneur is in perceiving opportunities—a skill gained through profession experience and entrepreneurial experience—the less uncertainty he/she will experience in the search process. Drawing again on Katila and Ahuja (2002, p. 1184):

> Increase in the depth of search can positively affect product innovation through three kinds of experience effects. First, using the same knowledge elements repeatedly reduces the likelihood of errors and false starts and facilitates the development of routines, making search more

---

[22]Of course, the set of opportunities in search areas A_2 through A_i may be different from each other. This concept thus implies that the effectiveness of a search, γ, should possibly have a time, t, subscript.

[23]I am assuming in this simple conceptual model that effectiveness does not vary across search areas, thus γ is not indexed. The symbols used in this model mirror those used in Leyden and Link (2015).

reliable...Increased experience is also likely to make a
search more predictable, as the knowledge to be searched is
familiar and the requirements the product should meet are
better understood...Third, repeated usage of a given set of
concepts can lead to significantly deeper understanding of
those concepts and boost a firm's ability to identify valuable
knowledge elements within them, to develop connections
among them, and to combine them in many different and
significant ways that are not apparent to less experienced
users of those concepts.

The notion that the effective use of new knowledge often involves
a recombination of that knowledge with existing knowledge traces to
Gilfillan (1935),[24] Usher (1955),[25] and to the more frequently quoted,
Schumpeter (1934, p. 78):[26, 27]

... everyone is an entrepreneur only when he actually 'carries
out new combinations,' and loses that character as soon as
he has built up his business, when he settles down to running
it as other people run their businesses.

---

[24]"The inventors are led by perceptions of the possibility and need of making
easily enough some recombinations of the 'prior art' and milieu" Gilfillan (1935,
p. 10).

[25]"In a formal theory of invention...it is possible to recognize four distinctive steps
in the process of invention: the perception of an unsatisfactory pattern, the setting of
the stage, the primary act of insight, and critical revision and development...After
the major act of insight has occurred, critical revision and development involve a
very intimate interweaving of minor acts of insight and acts of skill performed at
high levels by persons of special training...In considering the history of science and
technology, the acts of insight and the processes of cumulative synthesis that can
best be identified with invention are obviously more important than the acts of skill
which are performed in the current applications of knowledge to individual and social
needs" (Usher, 1955, pp. 527–529).

[26]Similarly, Nelson and Winter (1982, p. 130) wrote: "the creation of any sort
of novelty in art, science, or practical life-consists to a substantial extent of a
recombination of conceptual and physical materials that were previously in existence."
See also Fleming (2001) on combinations and uncertainty.

[27]Other notable scholars who have opined on the marriage of old and new technologies are Edgerton (2007) and Arthur (2009).

The relationship expressed by Equation (2.1) emphasizes the role of entrepreneurial experience with respect to search depth in search area A_1, but it does not address how search scope is related to P. How long an entrepreneur will search in area A_1 before completing his/her search or before moving into area A_2 involves what Simon (1957) called "bounded rationality."[28] An entrepreneur, searching area A_1 will not seek to maximize his/her utility or to maximize the probability-weighted value of P, rather, he/she will form a simplified model of a real situation in an effort to deal with it, meaning that he/she will stop searching in A_1 and/or will move on to area A_2 and then stop searching, etc., when he/she is satisfied with what has been learned. While not addressed in the extant literature, one might expect that an entrepreneur reaches a satisficing level of search based on his/her previous experiences.[29]

In the following Section 3, I describe the data that I use to approximate, although in a second best manner, the relationship between an entrepreneur's experience and his/her choice of a search area; and conditioned on the choice of a search area, I describe the data that I use to approximate the entrepreneur's efficiency in searching for new product innovation opportunities.

---

[28]Simon (1955) earlier used the terms "limited" rationality and "approximate" rationality" to contrast with "global" rationality or "classical" rationality.

[29]To conjecture, perhaps such experiences have been influenced by the scope of his/her social network and the strength of his/her relationships in the network. See Leyden and Link (2015) for a discussion of weak ties and strong ties to a social network based on the scholarship of Granovetter (1973) and Burt (2005).

3

The AEGIS Database

As emphasized in Section 1, this monograph departs from a traditional literature review in the sense that it uses aspects of the limited existing literature to motivate new research on theoretical models about the search for and use of alternative sources of knowledge and to motivate new research and empirical analyses of the consequences of the use of adopted knowledge. The data used for the empirical analyses are discussed here.

3.1 The AEGIS Project

The AEGIS (advancing knowledge-intensive entrepreneurship and innovation for growth and social well-being in Europe) project was funded by the European Commission (EC) under Theme 8 "Socio-Economic Sciences and Humanities" of the 7th Framework Programme (FP7) for Research and Technological Development.[1,2]

---

[1] See https://cordis.europa.eu/project/id/225134/reporting and the link to the full report therein.

[2] A description of the FP7 program is at: https://ec.europa.eu/commission/presscorner/detail/de/MEMO_16_146.

In Greek mythology, the word *Aegis* refers to the powerful shield carried by Athena and Zeus. Perhaps, or so I conjecture, titling the database with the name of the "AEGIS database" might imply that the database itself contains powerful information for an understanding of knowledge-intensive entrepreneurs and knowledge-intensive entrepreneurship.[3]

The objectives of the AEGIS project were three:[4]

> At the micro level, it purports to study in depth the very act of knowledge-intensive entrepreneurship, its defining characteristics, boundaries, scope and incentives. At the macro level, it will study the link between knowledge entrepreneurship, economic growth and social well-being, also extending to the socio-economic processes that help transform the "animal spirits" into a self-reinforcing process for broader societal prosperity...Finally, at the policy level, the project will take a systemic approach aiming at linking and integrating diverse sets of policies that influence the creation and growth of innovative entrepreneurial ventures based on knowledge generation and diffusion.

3.2 The AEGIS Database

The AEGIS database contains survey information, collected in 2010 and 2011, from young European entrepreneurial firms across 10 countries. All of these firms are younger than eight years (Malerba and McKelvey, 2019).[5] The countries represented in the sampling population are listed

---

[3]See Malerba and McKelvey (2019) for a masterful review of knowledge-intensive entrepreneurship (KIE).

[4]See   http://www.case-research.eu/en/aegis-advancing-knowledge-intensive-entrepreneurship-and-innovation-for-economic-growth-an-2.

[5]I appreciate Maribel Guerrero pointing out that the AEGIS data collected in 2010 and 2011 likely reflects some firm behavior in response to the Global Financial Crisis that had a significant effect on several European countries such as Greece, Italy, and Portugal. During this period entrepreneurs with more experience might have been better equipped to identify opportunities and implement different business strategies. The importance of an experience variable in the analyses that follow are thus important.

Table 3.1: Distribution of KIE firms, by country ($n = 4{,}004$)

Country	n
Croatia	200
Czech Republic	200
Denmark	330
France	570
Germany	557
Greece	331
Italy	580
Portugal	331
Sweden	334
United Kingdom	571
Sum	4,004

in Table 3.1 along with the number of KIE firms in each country that responded to the survey.[6]

The KIE firms in the AEGIS database can be grouped in several different ways. The KIE firms can be grouped in terms of the industries they represent. In addition to the countries in which that are geographically located. Table 3.2 shows the sampling population of firms by industry. It is clear from the table that the firms in the AEGIS database are not uniformly distributed across industrial sectors.

Finally, the sampling population of KIE firms can be grouped in a third way, namely by technology sector. Following Caloghirou *et al.* (2016), the high-tech sector could include aerospace; computers and office machinery; radio-television communication equipment; manufacture of medical, precision and optical instruments; pharmaceuticals; manufacturer of electrical machinery and apparatus, manufacturer of machinery and equipment, chemical industry. The low-tech sector could include paper and printing; textiles and clothing; food, beverage and tobacco; wood and furniture; basic metals; fabricated metal products.

---

[6]To account for the non-random sampling of firms, sampling weights were used, but our findings were similar with and without the use of the weights. The sampling weights are, by country: Croatia (11.985), Czech Republic (15.230), Denmark (23.909), France (100.249), Germany (66.470), Greece (12.628), Italy (89.371), Portugal (16.492), Sweden (62.533), and United Kingdom (21.764).

Table 3.2: Distribution of KIE firms, by industrial sector and by industry ($n = 4{,}004$)

NACE Code	n	Industrial Sector and Industry
		Manufacturing
15.00	297	Manufacture of food products and beverages
17.00	91	Manufacture of textiles
18.00	84	Manufacture of wearing apparel; dressing and dyeing of fur
19.00	34	Tanning and dressing of leather; manufacture of luggage, handbags, saddlery, harness and footwear
20.00	122	Manufacture of wood and of products of wood and cork, except furniture; manufacture of articles of straw and planting materials
21.00	46	Manufacture of pulp, paper and paper products
22.00	572	Publishing, printing and reproduction of recorded media
24.00	51	Manufacture of chemicals and chemical products
27.00	31	Manufacture of basic metals
28.00	214	Manufacture of fabricated metal products, except machinery and equipment
29.00	201	Manufacture of machinery and equipment n.e.c.
30.00	20	Manufacture of office machinery and computers
31.00	45	Manufacture of electrical machinery and apparatus n.e.c.
32.00	35	Manufacture of radio, television and communication equipment and apparatus
33.00	67	Manufacture of medical, precision and optical instruments, watches and clocks
35.30	1	Manufacture of aircraft and spacecraft
36.10	111	Manufacture of furniture
		Communication
64.20	24	Telecommunications
		Business Activities
72.00	518	Computer and related activities
73.00	71	Research and development

Continued.

Table 3.2: Continued.

NACE Code	*n*	Industrial Sector and Industry
74.10	767	Legal, accounting, book-keeping and auditing activities; tax consultancy; market research and public opinion polling; business and management consultancy; holdings
74.20	317	Architectural and engineering activities and related technical consultancy
74.30	60	Technical testing and analysis
74.40	116	Advertising
74.50	44	Labor recruitment and provision of personnel
74.80	65	Miscellaneous business activities n.e.c.

Table 3.3: Distribution of KIE firms, by technology sector ($n = 4{,}004$)

Sector	*n*
High-tech	420
Low-tech	1,602
Knowledge intensive business services	1,982
Sum	4,004

Note: See the text for a description of the industries in each of these sectors.

And knowledge-intensive business services (KIBS) sector could include telecommunications; computer and related activities; research and experimental development; selected business services activities. See Table 3.3.

Using these taxonomies, Table 3.4 shows the distribution of KIE firms by industrial sectors (i.e., manufacturing, communication, business activities) and by country.

And, Table 3.5 shows the distribution of KIE firms by technology sectors (i.e., high-tech, low-tech, and knowledge-intensive business services) and by country.

Table 3.4: Distribution of KIE firms across industrial sectors, by country ($n = 4{,}004$)

Country	Manufacturing Sector	Communication Sector	Business Activities Sector	Sum
Croatia	150	4	46	200
Czech Republic	117	0	83	200
Denmark	103	0	227	330
France	264	1	305	570
Germany	227	7	323	557
Greece	206	1	124	331
Italy	373	2	205	580
Portugal	201	0	130	331
Sweden	142	1	191	334
United Kingdom	239	8	324	571
Sum	2,022	24	1,958	4,004

Table 3.5: Distribution of KIE firms across technology sectors, by country ($n = 4{,}004$)

Country	High-Tech Sector	Low-Tech Sector	KIBS Sector	Sum
Croatia	35	115	50	200
Czech Republic	25	92	83	200
Denmark	34	69	227	330
France	68	196	306	570
Germany	67	160	330	557
Greece	22	184	125	331
Italy	57	316	207	580
Portugal	31	170	130	331
Sweden	34	108	192	334
United Kingdom	47	192	332	571
Sum	420	1,602	1,982	4,004

Note: KIBS refers to the knowledge-intensive business services.

In the following Section 4, I describe the 11 sources of knowledge considered in the AEGIS database by country, by industrial sector, and by technology sector.[7]

---

[7]I thank Conor O'Kane for pointing out that a limitation of using the AEGIS data, albeit a rich source of information on the sources of knowledge used by entrepreneurial firms, is that the data do not allow for quantifying lags in the adoption of alternative sources of knowledge and thus the ability to discern the use of multiple sources of knowledge over time is limited.

4

Sources of Knowledge

The AEGIS survey question that is the focus of the empirical analysis in this monograph is:

Please evaluate the importance of the following sources of knowledge for exploring new business opportunities on a 5 point scale, where 1 is not important and 5 is extremely important.

The "new business opportunities" considered in the exploratory empirical analysis in the following sections are assumed to relate to product innovation opportunities. This is a strong assumption because reason would suggest not all KIE firms pursue product innovation opportunities much less to the same degree. It is because of this maintained assumption that the empirical analysis in the following sections should be viewed as exploratory, and thus one effort at a correction is to condition the analyses in the following sections on country, industrial sector, and technology sector before offering any generalizations about the findings or about a roadmap for future research.

Table 4.1: Mean value of sources of knowledge used by KIE firms for exploring new business opportunities ($n = 4{,}004$)

Knowledge Source	Mean Value of Importance
Clients or customers	4.41
Suppliers	3.36
Competitors	3.27
Public research institutes	2.10
Universities	2.12
External commercial labs/R&D firms/technical institutes	2.04
In-house (know how, R&D laboratories in the firm)	3.27
Trade fairs, conferences and exhibitions	2.95
Scientific journals and other trade or technical publications	2.87
Participation in nationally funded research programs	1.90
Participation in EU funded research programs (framework programs)	1.87

Table 4.1 lists the 11 knowledge sources offered to the survey respondents along with mean importance value.[1] The highest ranked knowledge sources are market sources: clients or customers, suppliers, and competitors (tied with in-house know how). The lowest ranked sources are publicly funded research programs: participation in nationally funded research programs and participation in EU funded research programs (Framework Programs).

If one views a response value of 3.0 to the survey question to mean that the respondent and his/her firm is neutral about the importance of a particular source for exploring new business opportunities, then one interpretation of the mean values in Table 4.1 is that only four of the 11 sources are on average important and eight of the 11 sources are unimportant.

---

[1]This is not the first of my studies of these AEGIS survey questions about sources of knowledge. See, for example, in addition to Amoroso *et al.* (2018), Audretsch and Link (2019), Hodges and Link (2018), Link and Sarala (2019), and Link and Swann (2016).

Table 4.2: Mean value of sources of knowledge used by KIE firms for exploring new business opportunities, by country ($n = 4{,}004$)

Knowledge Source	Country									
	Croatia	Czech Republic	Denmark	France	Germany	Greece	Italy	Portugal	Sweden	United Kingdom
Clients or customers	4.40	4.15	4.38	4.30	4.34	4.29	4.43	4.76	4.44	4.54
Suppliers	3.75	3.14	3.01	3.26	3.04	3.63	3.69	4.13	3.03	3.18
Competitors	3.81	3.24	2.99	3.17	3.06	3.56	3.44	3.57	3.10	3.15
Public research institutes	2.68	1.72	1.92	1.85	1.87	2.37	2.37	2.60	1.90	2.02
Universities	2.69	1.74	1.86	1.77	2.07	2.36	2.34	2.87	2.00	1.85
External commercial labs/R&D firms/technical institutes	2.79	1.71	1.89	1.73	1.81	2.36	2.38	2.60	1.67	1.87
In-house (know how, R&D laboratories in the firm)	3.99	3.41	2.34	2.84	3.12	3.45	4.03	3.21	3.25	3.29
Trade fairs, conferences and exhibitions	3.71	2.85	2.63	2.45	3.10	3.15	3.06	3.40	2.75	2.89
Scientific journals and other trade or technical publications	3.64	2.84	2.56	2.50	3.08	2.95	2.94	3.15	2.86	2.71
Participation in nationally funded research programs	2.21	1.55	1.80	1.61	1.60	2.37	2.38	2.35	1.60	1.70
Participation in EU funded research programs (framework programs)	2.34	1.59	1.58	1.53	1.56	2.46	2.42	2.38	1.56	1.61

Table 4.3: Mean value of sources of knowledge used by KIE firms for exploring new business opportunities, by industrial sector ($n = 4{,}004$)

Knowledge Source	Industrial Sector		
	Manufacturing	Communication	Business Activities
Clients or customers	4.41	4.29	4.40
Suppliers	3.71	2.96	3.01
Competitors	3.40	3.46	3.14
Public research institutes	2.12	2.21	2.09
Universities	2.10	2.42	2.13
External commercial labs/R&D firms/technical institutes	2.13	2.30	1.95
In-house (know how, R&D laboratories in the firm)	3.29	3.38	3.25
Trade fairs, conferences and exhibitions	3.10	3.42	2.79
Scientific journals and other trade or technical publications	2.78	3.33	2.96
Participation in nationally funded research programs	1.93	1.96	1.86
Participation in EU funded research programs (framework programs)	1.94	1.92	1.80

Table 4.2 shows the mean important values for the 11 knowledge sources by country. In all countries, the highest valued knowledge source is clients or customers, but the next highest valued knowledge source varies across the countries. In Denmark, France, Greece, and Portugal the second highest valued knowledge source is suppliers. In Croatia, Czech Republic, Germany, Italy, Sweden, and the United Kingdom the second highest valued source is in-house knowledge: And, in general, the lowest valued sources are publicly funded research programs.

In Tables 4.3 and 4.4, the mean importance values for the 11 knowledge sources shows that whether one groups the information source data by industrial sector or by technology sector, the highest valued

Table 4.4: Mean value of sources of knowledge for exploring new business opportunities, by technology sector ($n = 4{,}004$)

	Technology Sector		
Knowledge Source	High-Tech Sector	Low-Tech Sector	Knowledge Intensive Business Services (KIBS)
Clients or customers	4.43	4.41	4.40
Suppliers	3.63	3.73	3.01
Competitors	3.34	3.41	3.14
Public research institutes	2.16	2.10	2.09
Universities	2.21	2.07	2.13
External commercial labs/R&D firms/technical institutes	2.18	2.11	1.95
In-house (know how, R&D laboratories in the firm)	3.44	3.25	3.25
Trade fairs, conferences and exhibitions	3.14	3.09	2.80
Scientific journals and other trade or technical publications	2.85	2.77	2.97
Participation in nationally funded research programs	2.08	1.89	1.86
Participation in EU funded research programs (framework programs)	2.05	1.91	1.80

knowledge source is clients or customers. And again, the lowest valued sources are again publicly funded research programs.

In the following Section 5, I describe the experience measure reported in the AEGIS database by country, by industrial sector, and by technology sector.

5

Measures of Experience

Building on the previously discussed (in Section 2) arguments of Locke that the search for knowledge is based on one's experiences and on the conceptualization of Audretsch and Link (2019) through their *Experience → Knowledge → Entrepreneurial Behavior* paradigm, the data used to quantify experience are discussed in this section.

The AEGIS survey question that relates to a KIE firm's entrepreneurial experience, where the firm's entrepreneur is defined to be a founder or founders of the firm, is based on a response(s) to the following survey question:

Approximately how many years of professional experience did the founder(s) have in the current sector your [firm] is active before the establishment of this [firm]?[1]

And, the AEGIS survey instrument asks this question for up to as many as four founders of a firm. The variable *ExperAll* refers to the

---

[1] The AEGIS survey used the word "company" rather than the word "firm."

Table 5.1: Mean years of experience of KIE firms, by country ($n = 4{,}004$)

Country	Mean Years of Experience
Croatia	17.04
Czech Republic	20.53
Denmark	18.71
France	21.83
Germany	24.47
Greece	28.34
Italy	27.90
Portugal	20.02
Sweden	22.58
United Kingdom	27.08

cumulative years of experience of all of the listed founders (information for a maximum of four founders is reported in the AEGIS database).[2,3]

Table 5.1 shows the mean values of this experience measure, by country. On average, the most experienced KIE firms are in Greece and the least experienced are in Croatia. Table 5.2 shows the mean values by industrial sector. On average, the experience base of KIE firms is similar across industrial sectors. And, Table 5.3 shows the mean values by technology sector. On average, the experience base is greater among KIE firms in the high-tech sector, and it is least among KIE firms in the KIBS sector.

Overall ($n = 4{,}004$), the mean value of this experience measure is 23.71 years.

---

[2]The mean number of founders is 2.03 with a range of 1 through 4. If this survey question was blank for the second, third, or fourth possible founder, then the value 0 was imputed so that a mathematical sum could be calculated to determine the number of founders in a KIE firm.

[3]The count method used to construct *ExperAll* does not take into account the distribution of years of experience across founders. In other words, if one KIE firm with one founder with 15 years of experience, and another KIE firm has three founders each with five years of experience, *ExperAll* equals 15 for both of the KIE firms.

Table 5.2: Mean years of experience of KIE firms, by industrial sector ($n = 4{,}004$)

Industrial Sector	Mean Years of Experience
Manufacturing	23.62
Communication	22.79
Business activities	23.80

Table 5.3: Mean years of experience of KIE firms, by technology sector ($n = 4{,}004$)

Industrial Sector	Mean Years of Experience
High-tech	28.93
Low-tech	23.79
Knowledge-intensive business services (KIBS)	22.26

6

Measures of Product Innovation Opportunities

The AEGIS survey question that asks about the sources of knowledge relevant to a KIE entrepreneur or a KIE firm is phrased in terms of new business opportunities rather than in terms of new product innovation opportunities: ... *the importance of the following sources of knowledge for exploring new business opportunities;* see Section 4. However, the AEGIS database does not include questions related to the *per se* pursuit of new business opportunities. Rather, the focus is on the realization of new business opportunities in terms of the market introduction of new or improved goods or services, which I am referring to as the realization of a product innovation opportunity.[1]

The relevant AEGIS survey question is:

> Did [your] company introduce new or significantly improved goods or services during the past three years? (Exclude the simple resale of new products purchased from other enterprises and changes of solely aesthetic nature).

---

[1]Caloghirou *et al.* (2016) state with regard to the AEGIS database survey question below: "Product innovation involves the introduction into the market of new or significantly improved products." And, they trace that interpretation of the OSLO Manual.

Table 6.1: Mean likelihood of a product innovation in the last three years, overall and by innovation type ($n = 4,004$)

Innovation	Mean Likelihood
Overall	0.64
New to the firm	0.41
New to the market	0.35
New to the world	0.14

And, the follow-on survey question is:

> [Was] the new or significantly improved goods or services new to [your] firm, new to the market, and/or new to the world?[2]

Table 6.1 shows the overall mean likelihood of an overall new product innovation and the mean likelihood of a product innovation by innovation type. Among product innovative KIE firms, that is firms that reported introducing a new or significantly improved goods or services to the market (2,548 of 4,004 KIE firms), 64 percent reported their product innovation being new to the firm, 55 percent reported their product innovation being new to the market, and 22 percent reported their product innovation being new to the world.

Table 6.2 replicates Table 6.1 with mean likelihood values, by country. Table 6.3 replicates Table 6.1 with mean likelihood values, by industrial sector. And, Table 6.4 replicates Table 6.1 with mean likelihood values, by technology sector.

From Table 6.1, 64 percent of KIE firms introduced a product innovation over the past three years. Most of those new goods or services (among the 4,004 KIE firms) were new to the firm or new to the market; only 14 percent were new to the world.

On a country by country basis, in Table 6.2, again most of the product innovations were new to the firm or new to the market. Only 5 percent of product innovations were new to the world in the Czech

---

[2]No precise definition of either new to the firm, new to the market, or new to the world is given in the AEGIS survey instrument.

Table 6.2: Mean likelihood of a product innovation in the last three years, by country and by innovation type ($n = 4{,}004$)

Country	Overall	Innovation Type		
		New to the Firm	New to the Market	New to the World
Croatia	0.69	0.61	0.50	0.12
Czech Republic	0.69	0.52	0.28	0.05
Denmark	0.59	0.26	0.35	0.13
France	0.54	0.31	0.31	0.12
Germany	0.60	0.41	0.38	0.14
Greece	0.70	0.58	0.41	0.10
Italy	0.74	0.44	0.38	0.15
Portugal	0.67	0.24	0.27	0.25
Sweden	0.62	0.43	0.34	0.15
United Kingdom	0.60	0.43	0.30	0.17

Table 6.3: Mean likelihood of a product innovation in the last three years, by industrial sector by innovation type ($n = 4{,}004$)

Industrial Sector	Overall	Innovation Type		
		New to the Firm	New to the Market	New to the World
Manufacturing	0.65	0.43	0.34	0.15
Communication	0.75	0.58	0.46	0.25
Business activities	0.62	0.38	0.36	0.14

Republic. Twenty-five percent of the product-innovation from KIE firms in Portugal were new to the world, about the same percent as were new to the firm or new to the market. Italy had the most product-innovative firms, with 74 percent of its KIE firms bringing a new product innovation to market in the last three years.

From Table 6.3, it appears that KIE firms in the communication industrial sector are the most product innovative, and 25 percent of those product innovations were new to the world.

And from Table 6.4, KIE firms in the high-tech sector are the most innovative with 70 percent being product innovative. KIE firms in the high-tech sector were also the most globally innovative, with 25 percent

Table 6.4: Mean likelihood of a product innovation in the last three years, by technology sector ($n = 4{,}004$)

Technology Sector	Overall	Innovation Type		
		New to the Firm	New to the Market	New to the World
High-tech	0.70	0.44	0.37	0.25
Low-tech	0.64	0.43	0.33	0.12
Knowledge-intensive business services (KIBS)	0.62	0.38	0.36	0.14

introducing product innovations in the last three years that were new to the world.

7

Experience and the Value of Alternative Knowledge Sources

In this section, I explore the relationship between entrepreneur's or a KIE firm's value of alternative knowledge sources (as defined in Section 4) used for product innovation opportunities and the experience base of the KIE firm (as defined in Section 5). The extant literature reviewed in Section 2 is suggestive of an hypothesis that experience leads an entrepreneur or a KIE firm to search first an area of possible relevant knowledge, and to continue to the next search area, and so on until the objective of the search process has been achieved.[1]

Even if each of the 11 listed knowledge sources represents a unique potential search area, the AEGIS database does not include variables that indicate which knowledge source was explored after and used first, second, and so on. Therefore, the best that one can glean from the AEGIS database is which knowledge sources appear to require experiential knowledge to exploit, given its perceived value to achieve new product innovation opportunities.

---

[1]I thank James Cunningham for reminding me that one of the reasons that entrepreneurs fail is that they fail to undertake sufficient market research to understand the opportunity(ies) sufficiently. So, their own experience and knowledge may lead to complacency that might mean that they fail to undertake any searches at all.

47

Table 7.1: Correlation coefficient between experience (*ExperAll*) and the value of knowledge sources ($n = 4{,}004$)

Knowledge Source	Correlation Coefficient
Clients or customers	0.017
Suppliers	−0.027*
Competitors	−0.005
Public research institutes	0.070***
Universities	0.053***
External commercial labs/R&D firms/technical institutes	0.063***
In-house (know how, R&D laboratories in the firm)	0.051***
Trade fairs, conferences and exhibitions	0.013
Scientific journals and other trade or technical publications	0.022
Participation in nationally funded research programs	0.031**
Participation in EU funded research programs (framework programs)	0.028*

Note: *** significant at 0.01-level, ** significant at 0.05-level, * significant at 0.10-level.

The correlation coefficients reported in Table 7.1 show that experiential knowledge is positively associated, in a statistical sense, with the use of six of the 11 sources of knowledge. Experiential knowledge is relatively more important for the use of knowledge sources from public research institutes, universities, external commercial labs/R&D firms/technical institutes, and in-house (know how, R&D laboratories in the firm). It is also important, but to a lesser extent when extracting product innovation knowledge, from publicly funded research programs.

As pointed out in Section 2, Criscuolo *et al.* (2018, p. 115) suggested that it might be optional for an entrepreneur or an entrepreneurial firm to search for a "combination of knowledge sources" to achieve an innovation opportunity. One possible way to utilize information in the AEGIS database toward an exploratory test of Criscuolo *et al.*'s hypothesis is to measure the use of a combination of knowledge sources as measured by the number of sources each entrepreneur or entrepreneurial

Table 7.2: Number of important knowledge sources used (*MultiUse*) and the correlation coefficient with experience (*ExperAll*), by country ($n = 4{,}004$)

Country	Number of Important Knowledge Sources Used (*MultiUse*)	Correlation Coefficient with Experience (*ExperAll*)
Croatia	6.29	−0.114
Czech Republic	3.90	−0.031
Denmark	3.73	0.031
France	3.91	0.023
Germany	4.30	0.083*
Greece	5.21	0.066
Italy	5.33	0.022
Portugal	5.64	0.022
Sweden	4.22	0.128**
United Kingdom	4.25	0.018

Note: *** significant at 0.01-level, ** significant at 0.05-level, * significant at 0.10-level.

firm values at greater than a response of 3.0 to the survey question.[2] I call this new variable *MultiSources*. For the 4,004 KIE firms represented in the AEGIS database, the mean value of this multi-source variable is 4.60, and the correlation between *MultiSources* and *ExperAll* is 0.037 ($p = 0.018$).

Table 7.2 shows the number of so defined important knowledge sources used for new product innovation opportunities and the correlation coefficient with that number, by country. Clearly, the number of sources used varies across countries from an average of just under four (Czech Republic, Denmark, France) to an average of more than six (Croatia). However, in general, the number of important knowledge sources used, with two exceptions, is not statistically correlated with the experience base of a KIE firm on a country by country basis.

---

[2]Recall that the AEGIS survey question asked for each of the 11 knowledge sources to be valued on a 5-point Likert scale from not important (=1) to extremely important (=5). One might interpret a value score of 3.0 as referring to a response that the specific knowledge source is knowledge neutral as a source for product innovation opportunities (i.e., neither important as a knowledge source or not important as a knowledge source).

Table 7.3: Number of important knowledge sources used (*MultiUse*) and the correlation coefficient with experience (*ExperAll*), by industrial sector ($n = 4{,}004$)

Industrial Sector	Number of Important Knowledge Sources Used (*MultiUse*)	Correlation Coefficient with Experience (*ExperAll*)
Manufacturing	4.77	0.050**
Communication	4.75	−0.256
Business activities	4.12	0.027

Note: *** significant at 0.01-level, ** significant at 0.05-level, * significant at 0.10-level.

Table 7.4: Number of important knowledge sources (*MultiUse*) used and the correlation coefficient with experience (*ExperAll*), by technology sector ($n = 4{,}004$)

Technology Sector	Number of Important Knowledge Sources Used (*MultiUse*)	Correlation Coefficient with Experience (*ExperAll*)
High-tech	4.90	0.069
Low-tech	4.74	0.041
Knowledge-intensive business services (KIBS)	4.20	0.291

Note: *** significant at 0.01-level, ** significant at 0.05-level, * significant at 0.10-level.

Tables 7.3 and 7.4 show the number of knowledge sources used for new product innovation opportunities, by industrial sector and by technology sector respectively. In all cases, the number was in the 4s, and in nearly all cases, with the exception of the manufacturing sector, the number of important knowledge sources used was not statistically correlated with the experience base of a KIE firm.

8

Correlates with Product Innovations: Descriptive Analyses

In this section, I quantify descriptively correlates with product innovation opportunities. In particular, I ask if the likelihood of a new product innovation (defined in Section 6) by a KIE firm varies with the experience base of the firm (defined in Section 5) and/or if it varies with the KIE firm's use of particular knowledge sources (defined in Section 4). A broad interpretation of the literature review in Section 2 suggests "yes" to both of these research questions. However, as I pointed out earlier, the AEGIS data are a second-best approximation of the concepts in the model described in Section 2, and to correct for that fact, analyses should, at a minimum, be conditioned on country, on industrial sector, and on technology sector. This section is a prelude to such a conditional analysis that follows in Section 9.

For ease of presentation of the descriptive correlates, all of the relevant concepts and variables are defined by name in Table 8.1. These variable names are used again in Sections 9 and 10.

From Table 8.2, it appears that a KIE firm's experience base is not related to, in a statistical sense, a KIE's likelihood of having a new product innovation either overall or by innovation type with the exception of a new product innovation that is new to the market. And,

51

Table 8.1: Definition of variables

Variable Name	Definition
Innov	=1 if the KIE firm introduced a new product innovation; 0 otherwise
NewFirm	=1 if the KIE firm introduced a new product innovation that was new to the firm; 0 otherwise
NewMarket	=1 if the KIE firm introduced a new product innovation that was new to the market; 0 otherwise
NewWorld	=1 if the KIE firm introduced a new product innovation that was new to the world; 0 otherwise
CumExper	Years of KIE firm founders' experiences in the same sector as the firm
Croatia	=1 if the KIE firm is in Croatia; 0 otherwise
CzechRep	=1 if the KIE firm is in Czech Republic; 0 otherwise
Denmark	=1 if the KIE firm is in Denmark; 0 otherwise
France	=1 if the KIE firm is in France; 0 otherwise
Germany	=1 if the KIE firm is in Germany; 0 otherwise
Greece	=1 if the KIE firm is in Greece; 0 otherwise
Italy	=1 if the KIE firm is in Italy; 0 otherwise
Portugal	=1 if the KIE firm is in Portugal; 0 otherwise
Sweden	=1 if the KIE firm is in Sweden; 0 otherwise
UK	=1 if the KIE firm is in the United Kingdom; 0 otherwise
Manuf	=1 if the KIE firm is in the manufacturing industrial sector; 0 otherwise
Commuc	=1 if the KIE firm is in the communication industrial sector; 0 otherwise
BussAct	=1 if the KIE firm is in the business activities industrial sector; 0 otherwise
HighTech	=1 if the KIE firm is in the high-tech technology sector; 0 otherwise
LowTech	=1 if the KIE firm is in the low-tech technology sector; 0 otherwise
KIBS	=1 if the KIE firm is in the knowledge-intensive business services technology sector; 0 otherwise
Client	=1 if the KIE firm used clients or customers as a knowledge source; 0 otherwise
Supply	=1 if the KIE firm used suppliers as a knowledge source; 0 otherwise

Continued.

Table 8.1: Continued.

Variable Name	Definition
Compet	=1 if the KIE firm used competitors as a knowledge source; 0 otherwise
PRI	=1 if the KIE firm used public research institutes as a knowledge source; 0 otherwise
Univ	=1 if the KIE firm used universities as a knowledge source; 0 otherwise
Labs	=1 if the KIE firm used external commercial labs/R&D firms/technical institutes as a knowledge source; 0 otherwise
R&D	=1 if the KIE firm used in-house (know how, R&D laboratories in the firm) as a knowledge source; 0 otherwise
Fairs	=1 if the KIE firm used trade fairs, conferences and exhibitions as a knowledge source; 0 otherwise
Jourl	=1 if the KIE firm used scientific journals and other trade or technical publications as a knowledge source; 0 otherwise
NatRes	=1 if the KIE firm used participation in nationally funded research programs as a knowledge source; 0 otherwise
EURes	=1 if the KIE firm used participation in EU funded research programs (framework programs) as a knowledge source; 0 otherwise
MultiUse	Number of knowledge sources used by the KIE firm
WomanOwned	=1 if all of the founders (up to four) of a KIE firm are women; 0 otherwise

Table 8.2: Correlation between product innovations and the experience base of KIE firms ($n = 4{,}004$)

	Innov	*NewFirm*	*NewMarket*	*NewWorld*
CumExper	0.022	0.017	0.038**	0.018

Note: *** significant at 0.01-level, ** significant at 0.05-level, * significant at 0.10-level.

the lack of such a relationship generally seems to hold on a country by country basis as shown in Table 8.3. The observed empirical exceptions are for Croatia, France, and Greece.

Table 8.3: Correlation between product innovations and the experience base of KIE firms, by country ($n = 4{,}004$)

Country	Product Innovations			
	Innov	*NewFirm*	*NewMarket*	*New World*
Croatia	0.083	0.057	0.130*	0.211***
CzechRep	−0.079	−0.026	0.034	0.051
Denmark	−0.049	0.027	−0.074	−0.001
France	0.001	−0.032	0.031	0.070*
Germany	−0.003	−0.053	0.046	0.013
Greece	0.149***	0.107*	0.145***	−0.011
Italy	0.002	0.016	0.044	0.008
Portugal	−0.012	0.002	0.056	−0.044
Sweden	0.031	0.070	0.006	0.002
UK	0.029	−0.034	−0.017	0.002

Note: *** significant at 0.01-level, ** significant at 0.05-level, * significant at 0.10-level.

Table 8.4: Correlation between product innovations and the experience base of KIE firms, by industrial sector ($n = 4{,}004$)

Industrial Sector	Product Innovations			
	Innov	*NewFirm*	*NewMarket*	*New World*
Manuf	0.049**	0.045**	0.073***	0.018
Commuc	−0.117	−0.305	−0.064	0.031
BussAct	−0.005	−0.010	0.001	0.017

Note: *** significant at 0.01-level, ** significant at 0.05-level, * significant at 0.10-level.

From Table 8.4, there appears to be a positive and statistically significant relationship between the experience base of a KIE firm in the manufacturing sector and the likelihood of an innovation overall. The same seems to be true for two types of innovations; an innovation that is new to the firm and an innovation that is new to the market. Similarly, in Table 8.5, there is a positive and statistically significant relationship between a firm in the high-tech sector and the likelihood of an innovation and an innovation new to the firm. In the low-tech sector, that relationship only shows up for an innovation that is new to the market.

Table 8.5: Correlation between product innovation measures and the experience base of KIE firms, by technology sector ($n = 4{,}004$)

Technology Sector	Product Innovations			
	Innov	*NewFirm*	*NewMarket*	*NewWorld*
HighTech	0.119**	0.148***	0.078	0.057
LowTech	0.021	0.013	0.067***	−0.024
KIBS	−0.006	−0.013	0.0003	0.017

Note: *** significant at 0.01-level, ** significant at 0.05-level, * significant at 0.10-level.

Perhaps the conclusion that one draws from the correlations presented in Table 8.6 is that new knowledge, from nearly any source, is a driver of innovative activity. Comparing the size of the correlation coefficients across knowledge sources suggest that sources rich in market-based knowledge (clients or customers, suppliers, and competitors) are less related (as measured by the size of the correlation coefficients) to the likelihood of innovative behavior than are sources

Table 8.6: Correlation between product innovations and the use of alternative knowledge sources by KIE firms ($n = 4{,}004$)

Knowledge Source	Product Innovations			
	Innov	*NewFirm*	*NewMarket*	*NewWorld*
Client	0.056***	0.004	0.026	0.010
Supply	0.040**	−0.001	0.033**	−0.013
Compet	0.073***	0.047***	0.036**	0.009
PRI	0.119***	0.050***	0.097***	0.088***
Univ	0.123***	0.041***	0.105***	0.122***
Labs	0.128***	0.055***	0.103***	0.097***
R&D	0.190***	0.107***	0.145***	0.111***
Fairs	0.161***	0.084***	0.115***	0.108***
Jourl	0.124***	0.072***	0.097***	0.070***
NatRes	0.150***	0.060***	0.115***	0.134***
EURes	0.140***	0.072***	0.096***	0.110***
MultiUse	0.166***	0.079***	0.129***	0.101***

Note: *** significant at 0.01-level, ** significant at 0.05-level, * significant at 0.10-level.

rich in technology-based knowledge. Of course, this suggested interpretation must be tempered because the AEGIS survey question related to the importance of a knowledge source was phrased: "... knowledge for exploring new business opportunities" and not about knowledge for developing new product innovations.

One might reasonably ask why, given the survey instrument's qualification for valuing a knowledge source, is that metric used in an analysis of new product innovation behavior. A glib response is that it is the best information available to study product innovativeness, and new product innovativeness is the conceptual metric to which the extant literature refers.

A more academic answer is that as insightful as is the extant *conceptual/theoretical* literature, the extant *empirical* literature related to the search for an use of new knowledge is nascent in its developments. As I posited in Section 1, the AEGIS database is arguably the most complete database dedicated exclusively to European entrepreneurial firms; knowledge-intensive innovative entrepreneurial (KIE) firms in particular. Using a conceptual/theoretical model based on the review of the extant literature in Section 2, the analyses presented in this section illustrate how far scholars can go with such data and thus how far scholars need to go to begin to understand more completely entrepreneurs' search for sources of knowledge.

9

Correlates with Product Innovations: Multivariate Analyses

This section expands on the descriptive analyses in Section 8 by using multivariate analyses. In particular, held constant in alternative regression models are country fixed effects, industrial sector fixed effects, and technology sector fixed effects.

Table 9.1 shows the Probit regression results of a model of the likelihood that a KIE firm will innovate, where innovation is defined in terms of the four variables *Innov*, *NewFirm*, *NewMarket*, and *NewWorld*. (See Table 8.1 for definitions of the variable in Table 9.1 and for the tables below.) Regardless of the innovation type, a KIE firm that uses multiple sources of knowledge is statistically more likely to innovate. However, the cumulative experience of the firm's founders is only positively and statistically related to the likelihood of having an innovation that is new to the market. This finding might be related to the observed fact that KIE firms' most highly valued sources of knowledge—clients or customers, suppliers, and competitors—are, on average, market oriented. Held constant in the model that underlies the specifications in Table 9.1 are country fixed effects.

The model that underlies the Probit regression results in Table 9.2 is the same as in Table 9.1 with the exception that held constant are

Table 9.1: Probit regression results from models of product innovation with country fixed effects ($n = 4{,}004$, marginal effects in brackets)

	Dependent Variable			
	Innov	*NewFirm*	*NewMarket*	*NewWorld*
CumExper	0.0007	0.0001	0.002**	0.001
			[0.0007]	
MultiUse	0.093***	0.035***	0.073***	0.068***
	[0.034]	[0.013]	[0.026]	[0.015]
Croatia	0.071	0.399***	0.385***	−0.373***
CzechRep	0.285***	0.252***	−0.037	−0.660***
Denmark	0.038	−0.426***	0.183**	−0.111
France	−0.113	−0.310***	0.045	−0.201**
Germany	−0.001	−0.030	0.218***	−0.139
Greece	0.189**	0.350***	0.219**	−0.402***
Italy	0.304***	−0.006	0.118	−0.155*
Portugal	0.082	−0.573***	−0.181	0.202**
Sweden	0.063	0.008	0.111	−0.062
Wald χ^2	149.65***	189.70***	108.90***	89.64***
Pseudo R^2	0.064	0.076	0.044	0.056
Log likelihood	−2547	−2607	−2534	−1592

Note: *** significant at 0.01-level, ** significant at 0.05-level, * significant at 0.10-level.

industrial sector fixed effects. And, the model that underlies the Probit regression results in Table 9.3 holds constant technology sector fixed effects. Again, the statistical driver of innovative activity is the use of multiple sources of knowledge.

Table 9.2: Probit regression results from models of product innovation with industrial sector fixed effects ($n = 4{,}004$, marginal effects in brackets)

	Dependent Variable			
	Innov	*NewFirm*	*NewMarket*	*NewWorld*
CumExper	0.001	0.001	0.002**	0.001
			[0.0007]	
MultiUse	0.102***	0.043***	0.077***	0.068***
	[0.037]	[0.017]	[0.028]	[0.015]
Manuf	−0.300	−0.389	−0.326	−0.392
BussAct	−0.344	−0.509*	−0.234	−0.418
Wald χ^2	113.83***	37.17***	75.80***	42.75***
Pseudo R^2	0.049	0.015	0.031	0.024
Log Likelihood	−2566	−2686	−2552	−1617

Note: *** significant at 0.01-level, ** significant at 0.05-level, * significant at 0.10-level.

Table 9.3: Probit regression results from models of product innovation with technology sector fixed effects ($n = 4{,}004$, marginal effects in brackets)

	Dependent Variable			
	Innov	*NewFirm*	*NewMarket*	*NewWorld*
CumExper	0.001	0.001	0.002**	0.0002
			[0.0007]	
MultiUse	0.102***	0.044***	0.077***	0.069***
	[0.037]	[0.017]	[0.028]	[0.015]
HighTech	0.167**	0.002	0.079	0.518***
KIBS	−0.006	−0.114***	0.112**	0.112**
Wald χ^2	117.39***	33.42***	76.14***	83.78***
Pseudo R^2	0.051	0.013	0.031	0.044
Log likelihood	−2564	−2688	−2551	−1597

Note: *** significant at 0.01-level, ** significant at 0.05-level, * significant at 0.10-level.

10

Nature versus Nurture and Product Innovations

As I discussed in Section 2, the extant literature emphasizes entrepreneur's and an entrepreneurial firm's experience as being relevant for the search for, identification of, and use of alternative sources of knowledge. This so-called nurture focus is perhaps most visible in the writings of Locke (1996, p. 33):

> Let us then suppose the mind to be, as we say, white paper, void of all characters, without any *ideas*; how comes it to be furnished? ... [I]n one word, from *experience*; in that, all our knowledge is founded ...

However, in Link and Morrison's (2019) literature review and in the review by Chowdhury *et al.* (2023), there is empirical evidence that women-owned firms are more innovative than men-owned firms in certain dimensions, controlling for the experience base of their firms. To extrapolate from this literature, I explore in this section the role of gender (i.e., so-called nature) in comparison to experience (i.e., so-called nurture) on the use of alternative sources of knowledge and on related new product innovations by KIE firms.

Overall, 7.69 percent of the 4,004 KIE firms in the AEGIS database are women owned as defined by all of the founders (up to four) of the firms being all women. Overall, 68.16 percent of the firms are all men owned as defined by all of the founders (up to four) of a firm being all men. The other 24.2 percent of the firms have a mix of women and men founders. Below I consider only a comparison between women-owned and men-owned firms ($n = 3{,}037$).

Table 10.1 shows the use of alternative knowledge sources by women-owned and by men-owned firms.[1] Clients or customers are a more valued source of knowledge for women-owned firms than for men-owned firms, but suppliers and competitors are equally valued between the two groups. These three sources of knowledge are market sources as emphasized in Section 9. There is also some visual evidence that men-owned firms value external technology-based sources of knowledge more highly than do women-owned firms. The mean value of the sources of universities, external commercial labs/R&D firms/technical institutes, participation in national funded research programs, and participation in EU funded research programs (Framework Programs) is greater for men-owned firms than for women-owned firms.[2]

As reported in Table 10.2, the cumulative years of experience of men-owned firms is nearly twice that of women-owned firms; 24.25 years versus 12.84 years. Although not reported in Table 10.2, this difference might be due to the fact that the mean number of founders of the sample of woman-owned firms is 1.32 compared to the mean number of founders of men-owned firms being 1.92. On a per founder basis, the mean cumulative years of experience per founder of woman-owned firms is 9.90 compared to 13.09 for men-owned firms.

Table 10.3 shows that men-owned firms are overall more new product innovative than women-owned firms. And the same relationship is observed empirically for new product innovations that are new to the market and new to the world.

Tables 10.4–10.6 show the Probit regression results from models of innovation, overall and by type, with the same specifications as in Tables 9.1–9.3, respectfully. The empirical findings from the three tables in this section mirror those from Section 9 with respect to the

---

[1]See also Menter (2022).
[2]Related to the issue of gender, see Goel *et al.* (2015).

Table 10.1: Sources of knowledge used by women-owned and men-owned KIE firms for exploring new business opportunities ($n = 3{,}037$)

	Mean Knowledge Importance Value	
Knowledge Source	Women-Owned Firms ($n = 308$)	Men-Owned Firms ($n = 2{,}729$)
Clients or customers	4.48	4.37
Suppliers	3.31	3.32
Competitors	3.29	3.23
Public research institutes	2.08	2.07
Universities	2.04	2.12
External commercial labs/R&D firms/technical institutes	1.90	2.03
In-house (know how, R&D laboratories in the firm)	3.15	3.28
Trade fairs, conferences and exhibitions	2.93	2.93
Scientific journals and other trade or technical publications	2.91	2.84
Participation in nationally funded research programs	1.75	1.89
Participation in EU funded research programs (framework programs)	1.79	1.85
MultiUse	4.61	4.53

Table 10.2: Mean years of experience of women-owned and men-owned KIE firms ($n = 3{,}037$)

	Women-Owned Firms	Men-Owned Firms
CumExper	12.84	24.25

relationship between the multiple use of sources of knowledge (*MultiUse*) and the likelihood of product innovation. In all cases, with the exception of product innovation that is new to the firm (*NewFirm*), nature seems to outperform, in a statistical sense, nurture as being a covariate with product innovation. In all cases, with the exception of the specification

Table 10.3: Product innovations, overall and by type, by woman-owned and men-owned KIE firms ($n = 3{,}037$)

Product Innovation	Women-Owned Firms	Men-Owned Firms
Innov	0.568	0.643
NewFirm	0.419	0.406
NewMarket	0.269	0.365
NewWorld	0.110	0.152

Table 10.4: Probit results of the likelihood of a product innovation by type by female-owned and male-owned KIE firms with country fixed effects ($n = 3{,}037$, marginal effects in brackets)

	Dependent Variable			
	Innov	*NewFirm*	*NewMarket*	*NewWorld*
CumExper	0.0002	−0.00002	0.002*	0.002
			[0.0007]	
MultiUse	0.095***	0.034***	0.076***	0.088***
	[0.034]	[0.013]	[0.028]	[0.020]
WomanOwned	−0.209***	0.025	−0.267***	−0.198*
Country effects	yes	yes	yes	yes
Wald χ^2	120.28***	135.59***	86.42***	92.41***
Pseudo R^2	0.068	0.071	0.047	0.075
Log likelihood	−1929	−1983	−1933	−1225

Note: *** significant at 0.01-level, ** significant at 0.05-level, * significant at 0.10-level.

with *NewFirm* as the dependent variable, the Probit coefficient on *WomanOwned* is negative and statistically significant.

Unfortunately, the analyses above do not conclusively resolve the relative importance of nature versus nurture when it comes to product innovation, but it does hint that nature might be more important.

Table 10.5: Probit results of the likelihood of a product innovation by type by female-owned and male-owned KIE firms with industrial sector fixed effects ($n = 3{,}037$, marginal effects in brackets)

	Dependent Variable			
	Innov	*NewFirm*	*NewMarket*	*NewWorld*
CumExper	0.0004	0.006	0.002*	0.001
			[0.0006]	
MultiUse	0.105***	0.046***	0.079***	0.082***
	[0.038]	[0.018]	[0.029]	[0.019]
WomanOwned	−0.208***	0.030	−0.254***	−0.198**
Industrial sector effects	yes	yes	yes	yes
Wald χ^2	92.75***	28.43	68.79	50.14
Pseudo R^2	0.053	0.015	0.037	0.036
Log likelihood	−1943	−2038	−1942	−1249

Note: *** significant at 0.01-level, ** significant at 0.05-level, * significant at 0.10-level.

Table 10.6: Probit results of the likelihood of a product innovation by type by female-owned and male-owned KIE firms with technology sector fixed effects ($n = 3{,}037$, marginal effects in brackets)

	Dependent Variable			
	Innov	*NewFirm*	*NewMarket*	*NewWorld*
CumExper	0.003	0.001	0.002	0.007
MultiUse	0.105***	0.011***	0.079***	0.083***
	[0.038]	[0.018]	[0.029]	[0.019]
WomanOwned	−0.199***	0.077	−0.249***	−0.155
Technology sector effects	yes	yes	yes	yes
Wald χ^2	94.76	26.99	68.72	79.06
Pseudo R^2	0.054	0.014	0.037	0.054
Log Likelihood	−1942	−2039	−1942	−1235

Note: *** significant at 0.01-level, ** significant at 0.05-level, * significant at 0.10-level.

11

Concluding Remarks

The purposes of this monograph are three: to explore the search process for knowledge by entrepreneurs and entrepreneurial firms in pursuit of new product innovation based on the academic and policy literatures, albeit that they are limited; to present empirical evidence about the sources of knowledge that entrepreneurs and entrepreneurial firms actually use in an effort to allow observed behavior to inform economics and management theory about the search for and use of knowledge; and to generate new and more complete empirical effort to construct database and to conduct analyses—empirical analyses and case studies—related not only to entrepreneur's and entrepreneurial firm's search for and use of sources of knowledge, but also to measure the trends in the impacts of their use.

My review of the extant literature related to entrepreneurs' search for sources of knowledge results in the conclusion that the literature is not only limited in its volume but also in its focus on the antecedents and consequences of the search for knowledge. In an effort to expand the theoretical and empirical aspects of the extant literature, information from the AEGIS database was used to illustrate empirically what is known about the use of alternative sources of knowledge about KIE firms. While the empirical analyses presented in several of the sections of this monograph are exploratory and first steps, they do suggest that future research on the topics at hand should focus on the use of portfolios of knowledge sources to understand better the innovative nature of KIE firms.[1] The role of the experience base of a KIE firm is still up in the air. I make this statement not only because of the limited statistical significance of the experience variable used herein, but also because there might be an interaction between nature and nurture; the experience base of women-owned KIE firms might not be comparable to the experience base of men-owned KIE firms.[2] This is an issue that is critically important, regardless of the speculative responses of some.[3]

Much remains to be learned about the search for sources of knowledge (their relevance as well as their accessibility) at both a theoretical level

---

[1]The analyses in Section 10 should be viewed as little more than a start in this direction.

[2]Perhaps one reason for the limited statistical significance of the experience variable is the lack of data to control for cross-country differences in the evolutional state of innovation ecosystems; an area for future study. See Audretsch *et al.* (2022). Another possible reason for the statistical insignificance of the experience variable is that the analyses do not consider whether an entrepreneur relies on individual sources of knowledge as compared to a changing portfolio of knowledge sources over time and in varying search areas.

[3]Chowdhury *et al.* (2023, p. 9) wrote about the finding that women-owned firms are less innovative than men-owned firms might be explained in terms of an informational trap. "Sen (2022, pp. 11–12) noted: Gender bias [can] limit the extent of appreciation that women scientists get, which can be a dampener, despite the growing involvement of women scientists in the actual work of medical research and in the operation of health systems. There is a serious issue of an "informational trap" in the contributions of women being much less acknowledged than they should be— biases in reporting can be very extensive … Furthermore, undercounting of female achievements also tends to discourage women from undertaking higher education and opting for "difficult and challenging" subjects of specialization … A second suggested answer to this question also relates to an informational deficiency, but not in terms of technical background *per se* but in terms of a deficiency in networks which might be an important source of technical information. Cook (2020, p. 15) noted: "Women and underrepresented minorities are less likely to be in the same innovation, commercialization, and entrepreneurship networks than their white male counterparts. Information that would help find and connect applicants to research partners, which is often exchanged in these networks, would be critical for them to obtain for their applications to be successful. This information is likely to be more difficult for them to access through unofficial means, and making it more publicly available could disproportionately help them."

and an empirical level. It might be the case that until future scholars lead us to understand better the knowledge creation to use process, public policies to enhance new product innovations and hence innovation-based economic growth will remain inside of a social frontier.

Acknowledgements

I appreciate the comments and suggestions from a number of individuals on earlier drafts of this monograph. Alphabetically, the scholars are David Audretsch, Maksim Belitski, James Cunningham, Rajeev Goel, Devrim Göktepe-Hultén, Maribel Guerrero, Matthias Menter, and Conor O'Kane. I am responsible for any remaining shortcomings in the monograph.

About the Author

Albert N. Link is the Virginia Batte Phillips Distinguished Professor at the University of North Carolina at Greensboro (UNCG). He received the B.S. degree in mathematics from the University of Richmond (Phi Beta Kappa) and the Ph.D. degree in economics from Tulane University. After receiving the Ph.D., he joined the economics faculty at Auburn University, was later Scholar-in-Residence at Syracuse University, and then he joined the economics faculty at UNCG in 1982. In 2019, Link was awarded the title and honorary position of Visiting Professor at Northumbria University, U.K.

Professor Link's research focuses on technology and innovation policy, the economics of R&D, and policy/program evaluation. He is currently the Editor-in-Chief of the *Journal of Technology Transfer*. He is also co-editor of *Foundations and Trends in Entrepreneurship* and founder and editor of *Annals of Science and Technology Policy*.

Among his more than 70 authored/co-authored and edited/co-edited books, some of the more recent ones are: *Small Firms and U.S. Technology Policy: Social Benefits of the US Small Business Innovation Research Program* (Edward Elgar, 2023), *Public Sector Entrepreneurship: Innovative Pricing Policies for U.S. National Parks* (Edward Elgar, 2022), *The Economics and Science of Measurement: A Study of Metrology* (Routledge, 2022), *Technology and Innovation Policy: An*

International Perspective (Edward Elgar, 2021), *Invention, Innovation and U.S. Federal Laboratories* (Edward Elgar, 2020), *Technology Transfer and U.S. Public Sector Innovation* (Edward Elgar, 2020), *Collaborative Research in the United States: Policies and Institutions for Cooperation among Firms* (Routledge, 2020), *Sources of Knowledge and Entrepreneurial Behavior* (University of Toronto Press, 2019), *Handbook for University Technology Transfer* (University of Chicago Press, 2015), *Public Sector Entrepreneurship: U.S. Technology and Innovation Policy* (Oxford University Press, 2015), *Bending the Arc of Innovation: Public Support of R&D in Small, Entrepreneurial Firms* (Palgrave Macmillan, 2013), *Valuing an Entrepreneurial Enterprise* (Oxford University Press, 2012), *Public Goods, Public Gains: Calculating the Social Benefits of Public R&D* (Oxford University Press, 2011), *Employment Growth from Public Support of Innovation in Small Firms* (W.E. Upjohn Institute for Employment Research, 2011), and *Government as Entrepreneur* (Oxford University Press, 2009).

Professor Link's other research endeavors consist of more than 250 peer-reviewed journal articles and book sections, as well as numerous U.S. government reports. His scholarship has appeared in such academic journals as the *American Economic Review*, the *Journal of Political Economy*, the *Review of Economics and Statistics*, *Economica*, *Research Policy*, *Economics of Innovation and New Technology*, the *European Economic Review*, *Small Business Economics*, *ISSUES in Science and Technology*, *Science and Public Policy*, *Scientometrics*, *IEEE Transactions on Engineering Management*, *International Entrepreneurship and Management Journal*, and the *Journal of Technology Transfer*.

Professor Link's public service includes being a member of the National Research Council's research team that conducted the 2010 evaluation of the U.S. Small Business Innovation Research (SBIR) program. Based on that assignment, he testified before the U.S. Congress in April 2011 on the economic benefits associated with the SBIR program. Link also served from 2007 to 2012 as a U.S. Representative to the United Nations (in Geneva, Switzerland) in the capacity of co-vice chairperson of the Team of Specialists on Innovation and Competitiveness Policies Initiative for the Economic Commission for Europe. In October 2018,

Link delivered the European Commission Distinguished Scholar Lecture at the European Commission's Joint Research Centre (in Seville, Spain).

Link served as a member of the National Institute of Standards and Technology (NIST) funded research team studying the economic impacts of investments in U.S. neutron research sources and facilities in 2022, and is an advisor to the research team focusing on the Phase IIB SBIR program in the National Heart, Lung, and Blood Institute within the Department of Health and Human Services in 2023 and 2024.

References

Amoroso, S., D. B. Audretsch, and A. N. Link (2018). "Sources of knowledge used by entrepreneurial firms in the european high-tech sector". *Eurasian Business Review.* 8: 55–70. DOI: 10.1007/s40821-017-0078-4.

Arthur, W. B. (2009). *The Nature of Technology: What it is and How it Evolves.* New York: Free Press.

Audi, R. (2002). "The sources of knowledge". In: *The Oxford Handbook of Epistemology.* Ed. by P. K. Moser. New York: Oxford University Press. 71–94.

Audretsch, D. B. and M. Belitski (2020). "The role of R&D and knowledge spillovers in innovation and productivity". *European Economic Review.* 123: 103391. DOI: 10.1016/j.euroecorev.2020.103391.

Audretsch, D. B. and M. Belitski (2021). "Frank Knight, uncertainty and knowledge spillover entrepreneurship". *Journal of Institutional Economics.* 17: 1005–1031. DOI: 10.1017/S1744137421000527.

Audretsch, D. B. and M. Belitski (2023). "The limits to open innovation and its impact on innovation performance". *Technovation.* 119: 102519. DOI: 10.1016/j.technovation.2022.102519.

Audretsch, D. B., M. Belitski, R. Caiazza, and D. Siegel (2023). "Effects of open innovation in startups: Theory and evidence". *Technological Forecasting and Social Change.* 194: 122694. DOI: 10.1016/j.techfore.2023.122694.

Audretsch, D. B., M. Belitski, and M. Guerrero (2022). "The dynamic contribution of innovation ecosystems to schumpeterian firms: A multi-level analysis". *Journal of Business Research*. 144: 975–986. DOI: 10.1016/j.jbusres.2022.02.037.

Audretsch, D. B. and A. N. Link (2019). *Sources of Knowledge and Entrepreneurial Behavior*. Toronto: University of Toronto Press.

Billinger, S., K. Srikanth, N. Stieglitz, and T. R. Schumacher (2021). "Exploration and exploitation in complex search tasks: How feedback influences whether and where human agents search". *Strategic Management Journal*. 42: 361–385. DOI: 10.1002/smj.3225.

Bradley, S. R., C. S. Hayter, and A. N. Link (2013). "Models and methods of university technology transfer". *Foundations and Trends in Entrepreneurship*. 9: 571–650. DOI: 10.1561/0300000048.

Burt, R. S. (2005). *Brokerage and Closure: An Introduction to Social Capital*. Oxford: Oxford University Press.

Caloghirou, Y., A. Protogerou, and A. Tsakanikas (2016). "The AEGIS survey: A quantitative analysis of new entrepreneurial ventures in Europe". In: *Dynamics of Knowledge Intensive Entrepreneurship: Business Strategy and Public Policy*. Ed. by Y. Malerba, Y. Caloghirou, M. McKelvey, and S. Radosevic. London: Routledge. 48–94.

Chowdhury, F., A. N. Link, and A. B. Royalty (2023). "Gender and innovation at the US National Institutes of Health". *Small Business Economics*. DOI: 10.1007/s11187-023-00740-y.

Cook, L. D. (2020). *Policies to Broaden Participation in the Innovation Process*. The Hamilton Project Policy Proposal, The Brookings Institution.

Criscuolo, P., K. Laursen, T. Reichstein, and A. Salter (2018). "Winning combinations: Search strategies and innovativeness in the UK". *Industry and Innovation*. 25: 115–143. DOI: 10.1080/13662716.2017. 1286462.

Edgerton, D. (2007). *The Shock of the Old: Technology and Global History Since 1900*. New York: Oxford University Press.

Fleming, L. (2001). "Recombinant uncertainty in technological search". *Management Science*. 47: 117–132. DOI: 10.1287/mnsc.47.1.117. 10671.

Foss, N. J. and P. G. Klein (2012). *Organizing Entrepreneurial Judgment: A New Theory of the Firm*. Cambridge: Cambridge University Press.

Gilfillan, S. C. (1935). *The Sociology of Invention*. Chicago, IL: Follett Publishing Company.

Goel, R. K., D. Göktepe-Hultén, and R. Ram (2015). "Academics' entrepreneurship propensities and gender differences". *Journal of Technology Transfer*. 40: 161–177. DOI: 10.1007/s10961-014-9372-9.

Goel, R. K. and M. Nelson (2018). "Determinants of process innovation introduction: Evidence from 115 developing counties". *Managerial and Decision Economics*. 39: 515–525. DOI: 10.1002/mde.2922.

Goel, R. K. and D. Rich (2005). "Organization for markets for science and technology". *Journal of Institutional and Theoretical Economics*. 161: 1–17. DOI: 10.1628/0932456054254489.

Granovetter, M. S. (1973). "The strength of weak ties". *The American Journal of Sociology*. 78: 1360–1380. DOI: 10.1086/225469.

Guerrero, M. and I. Peña-Legazkue (2013). "The effect of intrapreneurial experience on corporate venturing: Evidence from developed economies". *International Entrepreneurship and Management Journal*. 9: 397–416. DOI: 10.1007/s11365-013-0260-9.

Hayter, C. S., A. N. Link, and J. T. Scott (2018). "Public-sector entrepreneurship". *Oxford Review of Economic Policy*. 4: 676–694. DOI: 10.1093/oxrep/gry014.

Hébert, R. F. and A. N. Link (2009). *A History of Entrepreneurship*. Oxford, UK: Routledge.

Hodges, N. J. and A. N. Link (2018). *Knowledge-Intensive Entrepreneurship an Analysis of the European Textile and Apparel Industries*. Cham, Switzerland: Springer Nature.

Johnson, S. (2010). *Where Good Ideas Come From: The Natural History of Innovation*. New York: Penguin Group.

Jung, H. J. and J. J. Lee (2016). "The quest for originality: A new typology of knowledge search and breakthrough inventions". *The Academy of Management Journal*. 59: 1725–1753. DOI: 10.5465/amj.2014.0756.

Katila, R. (2002). "New product search over time: Past ideas in their prime?" *The Academy of Management Journal*. 45: 995–1010. DOI: 10.2307/3069326.

Katila, R. and G. Ahuja (2002). "Something old, something new: A longitudinal study of search behavior and new product introduction". *The Academy of Management Journal*. 45: 1183–1194. DOI: 10.2307/3069433.

Katila, R. and E. L. Chen (2008). "Effects of search timing on innovation: The value of not being in sync with rivals". *Administrative Science Quarterly*. 53: 593–625. DOI: 10.2189/asqu.53.4.593.

Kirzner, I. M. (1985). *Discovery and the Capitalist Process*. Chicago, IL: University of Chicago Press.

Knight, F. H. (1921). *Risk, Uncertainty and Profit*. New York: Houghton Mifflin.

Krueger Jr., N. F., M. D. Reilly, and A. L. Carsrud (2000). "Competing models of entrepreneurial intentions". *Journal of Business Venturing*. 15: 411–432. DOI: 10.1016/S0883-9026(98)00033-0.

Laursen, K. and A. Salter (2006). "Open for innovation: The role of openness in explaining innovation performance among U.K. Manufacturing Firms". *Strategic Management Journal*. 27: 131–150.

Leventhal, D. A. and J. G. March (1993). "The myopia of learning". *Strategic Management Journal*. 14: 95–112. DOI: 10.1002/(ISSN) 1097-0266.

Leyden, D. P. and A. N. Link (2015). "Toward a theory of the entrepreneurial process". *Small Business Economics*. 44: 475–484. DOI: 10.1007/s11187-014-9606-0.

Leyden, D. P. and M. Menter (2018). "The legacy and promise of Vannevar Bush: Rethinking the model of innovation and the role of public policy". *Economics of Innovation and New Technology*. 27: 225–242.

Leyden, D. P. and M. Menter (2022). "The impact of knowledge on innovation: Exploiting the cross-fertilization of basic and applied research". In: *Handbook of Technology Transfer*. Cheltenham, UK and Northampton, MA: Edward Elgar.

Li, Q., P. G. Maggitti, K. G. Smith, P. E. Tesluk, and R. Katila (2013). "Top management attention to innovation: The role of search selection and intensity in new product introductions". *The Academy of Management Journal*. 56: 893–916. DOI: 10.5465/amj.2010.0844.

Link, A. N. (2020). *Invention, Innovation, and U.S. Federal Laboratories.* Cheltenham, UK and Northampton, MA: Edward Elgar.

Link, A. N. and L. T. R. Morrison (2019). *Innovative Activity in Minority-Owned and Women-Owned Business: Evidence from the U.S. Small Business Innovation Research Program.* Cham, Switzerland: Springer.

Link, A. N. and R. M. Sarala (2019). "Advancing conceptualisation of university entrepreneurial ecosystems: The role of knowledge-intensive entrepreneurial firms". *International Small Business Journal.* 37: 289–310. DOI: 10.1177/0266242618821720.

Link, A. N. and C. A. Swann (2016). "R&D as an investment in knowledge based capital". *Economia e Politica Industriale: Journal of Industrial and Business Economics.* 43: 11–24. DOI: 10.1007/s40812-015-0024-3.

Locke, J. (1996). *An Essay Concerning Human Understanding.* Ed. by K. P. Winkler. Cambridge, MA: Hackett Publishing Company.

Machlup, F. (1980). *Knowledge and Knowledge Production.* Princeton, NJ: Princeton University Press.

Malerba, F. and M. McKelvey (2019). "Knowledge-intensive innovative entrepreneurship". *Foundations and Trends in Entrepreneurship.* 14: 555–681. DOI: 10.1561/0300000075.

March, J. G. (1991). "Exploration and exploitation in organizational learning". *Organization Science.* 2: 7–87. DOI: 10.1287/orsc.2.1.71.

Menter, M. (2022). "Entrepreneurial universities and innovative behavior: The impact of gender diversity". *Economics of Innovation and New Technology.* 37: 20–34.

Nelson, R. R. and S. G. Winter (1982). *An Evolutionary Theory of Economic Change.* Cambridge, MA: Belknap Press.

Radner, R. and M. Rothschild (1975). "On the allocation of effort". *Journal of Economic Theory.* 10: 358–376. DOI: 10.1016/0022-0531(75)90006-X.

Rosenkopf, L. and A. Nerkar (2001). "Beyond local search: Boundary-spanning, exploration, and impact in the optical disk industry". *Strategic Management Journal.* 22: 287–306. DOI: 10.1002/(ISSN)1097-0266.

Sarasvathy, S. D. (2001). "Causation and effectuation: Toward a theoretical shift from economic inevitability to entrepreneurial contingency". *Academy of Management Review*. 26: 243–263. DOI: 10.2307/259121.

Schultz, T. W. (1975). "The value of the ability to deal with disequilibria". *Journal of Economic Literature*. 13: 827–846.

Schumpeter, J. A. (1928). "The instability of capitalism". *Economic Journal*. 38: 361–386. DOI: 10.2307/2224315.

Schumpeter, J. A. (1934). *The Theory of Economic Development*. Translated by R. Opie from the 2nd German edition [1926]. Cambridge, MA: Harvard University Press.

Sen, A. (2022). "Women scientists and pandemics". *Economia Politica*. 39: 7–14. DOI: 10.1007/s40888-021-00244-6.

Simon, H. A. (1955). "A behavioral model of rational choice". *Quarterly Journal of Economics*. 69: 99–118. DOI: 10.2307/1884852.

Simon, H. A. (1957). *Models of Man: Social and Rational-Mathematical Essays on Rational Human Behavior in a Social Setting*. New York: John Wiley & Sons.

Stuart, T. E. and J. M. Podolny (1996). "Local search and the evolution of technological capabilities". *Strategic Management Journal*. 17: 21–38. DOI: 10.1002/smj.4250171004.

Usher, A. P. (1955). "Technical change and capital formation". In: *Capital and Economic Growth*. Princeton, NJ: Princeton University Press for the National Bureau of Research. 523–550.

von Mises, L. (1949). *Human Action: A Treatise on Economics*. New Haven, CT: Yale University Press.

von Wieser, F. (1927). *Social Economics*. Ed. by A. F. Hindrichs. New York: Adelphi.

Milton Keynes UK
Ingram Content Group UK Ltd.
UKHW020636271123
433341UK00011B/853